Tennessee Williams

Titles in the series Critical Lives present the work of leading cultural figures of the modern period. Each book explores the life of the artist, writer, philosopher or architect in question and relates it to their major works.

In the same series

Tennessee Williams

Paul Ibell

REAKTION BOOKS

For Tom Erhardt

Published by Reaktion Books Ltd
Unit 32, Waterside
44–48 Wharf Road
London N1 7UX, UK
www.reaktionbooks.co.uk

First published 2016
Copyright © Paul Ibell 2016

Printed and bound in Great Britain by Bell & Bain, Glasgow

A catalogue record for this book is available from the British Library

ISBN 978 1 78023 662 9

Contents

Tennessee Williams at the 20th anniversary of *The Glass Menagerie* opening, 1965.

Foreword

Thomas Lanier Williams III (1911–1983) is America's greatest playwright, but his legacy of work belongs to the world. He is popular across the globe – in Western Europe, Russia and the Far East, as well as the United States – because his plays, though often set in the Deep South, have a European sensibility and a universal appeal.

This comes from the themes that are central to his most enduring works: sexual desire, nostalgia for lost youth and beauty, the importance of money, and the conflict between what we hope for in life and what it actually delivers. His ability to create memorable, impressive, yet sympathetically vulnerable female roles is a particular strength. He also overturns conventional concepts of masculinity by taking what have traditionally been thought of as female concerns – the loss of youth and beauty referred to above – and making them central to the personal tragedies of some of his leading male characters.

There have been a great many books – and an avalanche of articles – about Tennessee Williams, but, as with all great artists, the raw material of his life and the work through which he expressed himself repay any number of visits, whether by biographers or those primarily interested in his plays. These two inevitably overlap, as there can be no other playwright who so resolutely and imaginatively mined his family, his sex life and his neuroses for material. Though his work gathered many laurels, he was never content to rest upon them: he spent over forty years writing for the stage. Inevitably, during that period and in the decades since, theatrical tastes have changed, but he has never gone out of fashion. Even when his new works were being rubbished, his masterpieces were acknowledged and performed. Whether early (*The Glass Menagerie*; *A Streetcar Named Desire*) or late (*Something Cloudy, Something Clear*; *Vieux Carré*), his work compellingly portrays human frailties and our often doomed attempts to rise above them.

For someone so dedicated to art and so contemptuous of commerce, his writing displays an astute awareness of the importance of money. In his understanding of the world it formed part of a secular trinity, along with youth and good looks. Everyone eventually loses the last two, and many fail to hang on to their cash – especially in the age in which he grew up, which saw the Wall Street Crash of 1929 and the Depression, when many lost the wealth that had once defined them. F. Scott Fitzgerald (who, with his wife Zelda, is at the heart of Williams's play *Clothes for a Summer Hotel*) wrote about the young, talented and wealthy who, despite these advantages, had crises of their own. Williams, by contrast, showed us the no-longer young, those without money or a bankable talent in an American South whose obsession with social class mirrored the European societies that had, in colonial times, established its cities, its architecture and the origins of its social mores.

Like other great American authors between the wars – specifically, Fitzgerald and Ernest Hemingway – Williams was an American fascinated by Europe, but he was drawn to Italy and the myths of the classical world rather than to Fitzgerald's France or Hemingway's Spain. Whereas previous Americans, headed by Henry James, had concentrated on the upper strata of a European society at its zenith, Tennessee Williams saw a continent shattered by two devastating wars – and was in any case interested in the damaged but decorative rather than the confident and comfortably off. It is telling that the beautiful male prostitute, Paolo, in *The Roman Spring of Mrs Stone*, is not a street youth but from an aristocratic family, destitute after the Second World War.

The Italian setting of that novella, and influence in his play *The Rose Tattoo* (both later filmed), was again a mixture of professional and personal – influenced by his relationship with an Italian-American lover, Frank Merlo, and by his many visits to Italy, especially in the 1940s and 1950s, when he made full use of the combined beauty and poverty of young Italian males.

His emotional engagement with Italy has been repaid by Europe's fascination with his plays, hence his popularity across the Continent, including in Russia: he admired and was influenced by Anton Chekhov. Some of his heroines – damaged, drifting – have a similar sensibility to those of Chekhov's: middle-aged women, in thrall to hopelessly unsuitable men, wholly unable to deal with real life and wilfully refusing to accept the help that is offered. Arcadina's cherry orchard, in the play of that name, and the DuBois' lost mansion Belle Reve in *A Streetcar Named Desire,* may have been thousands of miles apart, but they are closely related, which is one reason why Williams earned a fortune in the Soviet Union. Audiences there enjoyed the escapism of plays set in the American South but were able to empathize with his characters.

Williams's appeal, enhanced by interest in the autobiographical elements of the characters he so vividly brings to life in his plays, has continued into our own age, during which established artists and wannabes alike don't so much wear their hearts on their sleeves as hand them over, bleeding and beating, on camera. Fascination with everyone's personal life means that, no longer content with watching them (or their work) onstage, we want to see stars naked, without make-up or in their dressing rooms – preferably throwing up into a sink with pre-performance nerves or reaching for wine, whisky or a range of pharmaceutical products to get through the show. The tears of a clown are no longer poignant enough for us. We want their heart-wrenching sobs.

With Williams's work, audiences can reflect, either with empathy or with schadenfreude, on how their own lives are so much less turbulent, less tortured, than those of the people onstage and the playwright who created them. He may have had fame and fortune, they can tell themselves as they head off to a restaurant for a post-theatre dinner or read the programme notes on the way home, but he was so very satisfactorily unhappy – as befits an artist. For if artists aren't going to die young, poor and as yet undiscovered, like the teenage poet Thomas Chatterton, or the thirty-something Vincent Van Gogh, then they should at least have the decency, like Judy Garland or Edith Piaf, to have the pairing of a transcendent talent with a messy and ultimately disastrous private life.

Tennessee Williams fits this profile perfectly, his childhood and adolescence effortlessly embodying Philip Larkin's assertion that your parents f*** you up. Along with alcoholism, drug addiction and madness (little wonder his plays often have more than a touch of opera to them) Williams's adult life was one of promiscuous sex. Sexuality – its power, its cost and the lack of dignity and self-respect that accompany it as one ages – is a constant theme in his plays. Despite this, those same dramas recognize the inevitability of sexual attraction and the life force that it represents, even when its expression is doomed, as in *Something Cloudy, Something Clear*: 'How goddam stupid it is to look at them with envy, the perfect ones, the ones that appear to be completely, completely flawless, the – perfect – with eyes like startled flowers . . .'

The link between his art and his sex life was one he was unnervingly open about. How many other literary autobiographies, for example, have, as in his memoirs, casually thrown in advice as to the best pesticide to deal with pubic lice? And how many other writers have been so self-coruscating in their work, showing the worst side of themselves, as he did, in both male and female characters? The inevitable traumas that accompanied his lifestyle were part of the price he paid for it, but they were also the raw material for his art. One of his plays was titled *I Rise in Flame, Cried the Phoenix.* Since his death, his art has risen from the ashes that once obscured the full range of his genius, and this book looks not just at his life and career but at his posthumous artistic revival.

For generations of theatre audiences, Williams has been synonymous with an overheated atmosphere of sex, sun and the American South. His world is one of faded beauties, sweaty masculinity and wrecked dreams. He is the poet laureate of life's failures: the moths whose wings were fatally burned. Indeed, one of his best-known plays, *A Streetcar Named Desire*, was going to be called *The Moth* until his sense of poetry, which produced a string of haunting titles, won the day. If his name still guarantees interest from the twenty-first-century ticket-buying public, it also attracts the ambitions of actors, offering as it does some of the greatest roles (especially for middle-aged women) in Western theatre. Unsurprising, then, that more than thirty years after his death, and some fifty years after contemporary critics seemed to write him off as a has-been, he and his works continue to be a vital, award-winning and much-loved part of the theatre world.

This book looks at the process by which Tennessee Williams transferred his experiences, interests and imagination, via his typewriter, onto the stage, using the proscenium arch as a frame within which to display the essential tragedy – punctuated by wit and occasional joy – of the human condition.

Tennessee Williams's unhappily married parents, Cornelius and Edwina. Though as a child Tennessee was far closer to his mother, he came to dislike her in later life. Cornelius is usually seen as the villain of the family situation, but he had his excuses and, though Tennessee would not like to admit it, father and son had a lot in common.

1

Early Life

Tennessee Williams had a lucky start in life: his family was perfect material for a playwright who specialized in the damaged and the doomed. Born on 26 March 1911 in Columbus, Mississippi, to Edwina (née Dakin) and the unpromisingly named Cornelius Coffin Williams, Thomas Lanier Williams III was from a relatively well-bred background. His status-conscious mother's efforts to cling to some sort of gentility in reduced circumstances proved good material for the writer in years to come, but they antagonized his father, a salesman (and latterly executive) who took refuge in drink and in work that frequently took him away from a family that, eventually, comprised the unhappy couple and three children: Rose (1909–1996), Tom (1911–1983) and Dakin (1919–2008).

Once it was clear, in his late twenties, that he had a talent as a playwright, Tom adopted the name Tennessee. It has been suggested that this was originally a nickname, based on his Southern drawl, given to him by his fellow students at university, but it is just as likely that he chose it himself. It has several advantages over his birth name of Thomas – or Tom, as the family called him. Grander American families often gave their children surnames as Christian names (as was the case with his friend Gore Vidal) and indeed Tennessee's younger brother was given his mother's maiden name. Tom went one stage further, calling himself not after a family, but a state. It is highly distinctive, which is always helpful for a writer, especially one with a commonplace surname. It is also, by definition, redolent of the South, an area that once belonged to Mark Twain and Margaret Mitchell, but which was to become forever identified with Tennessee Williams's plays and the films that were made of them. It has a poetic ring, too, which is appropriate for a playwright whose dialogue is often close to poetry, who wrote verse and indeed saw himself as a poet. Much as he admired Anton Chekhov, his greatest literary hero was the American poet Hart Crane. Williams's desire to be buried at sea, preferably near the spot where Crane slipped beneath the waves in an apparent suicide, was not fulfilled – but his tombstone in St Louis, Missouri, credits him as a poet first and a playwright second.

An irony in his choice of name was that it was associated with his father's rather than his mother's side of the family. Though it was his mother who was class conscious, it was his father who had the grander social background, being related to one of the founders of the state of Tennessee. Williams did not get on with his father, who believed his oldest son to be a disappointment. He had wanted a classic American boy, who played sports and chased girls. After a childhood illness that nearly killed the boy, cost him the use of his legs for some two years and led to a change in his personality from relatively outgoing to distinctly shy and withdrawn, what Cornelius got was a sickly bookworm who lived in the imagination rather than on the sports field and whose closest relationships were with his mother and sister, rather than his father and younger brother. These characteristics, along with a delicate, almost feminine, sensibility irritated Cornelius, who contemptuously referred to his eldest son as 'Miss Nancy'.

This dislike was entirely mutual. Taking the name Tennessee was not a sign of filial devotion. It was, rather, a defiant appropriation of that side of his family background – a staking of his own claim to a heritage of achievement that his father failed to live up to. It was not a tribute to his father; it was a snub. Cornelius has generally been seen, understandably, as the villain of the family situation, but given that the woman he married turned out to be a neurotic, son-smothering hysteric, whose almost manic chatter would try anyone's patience (Tennessee joked, in later life, that his mother would no doubt continue to talk, on a sort of autopilot, half an hour after she was placed in her coffin), one cannot help, however much one identifies with the tortured artistry of his eldest son, but have some sympathy with the father.

Cornelius's brutish behaviour towards his family was far from admirable, but if the losers in life deserve some understanding, as Tennessee's plays so often argued, then perhaps Cornelius should be shown a little, too. For although he was a difficult and unsympathetic type to his wife and eldest children, a Big Daddy without that character's money or prestige, he was no less damaged or unhappy. That he was capable of affection was shown by his relatively straightforward and amiable relationship with his youngest son, Dakin. Similarly, Tennessee's later problems with drink and drugs are, like those of all such artists, generally regarded in a sympathetic light by commentators and fans. If addiction is to be pitied, then surely the same courtesy should be shown to the alcoholic and unhappy father.

Cornelius enjoyed the company of other women, especially on his business travels, but this was as much a reaction to the lack of sexual and emotional comfort he received from his wife as it was a heartless philandering. Indeed, it was the heart that led to the philandering, having received so little exercise at home. Edwina had a puritan streak in her that cannot be explained simply by reference to her father's profession as a rector. It is more common for children of clergymen to embrace sensuality as a reaction against their parents. Yet here the roles were somewhat reversed. Edwina's father, the Reverend Walter Dakin, was high church in his worship and something of a man of the world. He had no difficulty with his grandson's homosexuality and in old age was to live with him in Key West, taking the presence of Williams's male lover entirely in his stride.

Edwina's issues with sex were down to her own personality, rather than her upbringing. According to her son, she would scream when her husband had sex with her – a cry not of pleasure but of indignation and disgust at an act she found animal and upsetting. Hardly surprising, then, that her husband found solace elsewhere, albeit in less than salubrious surroundings.

Tennessee, very much his mother's son in terms of family allegiance and affection, was in adult life to take after his father in more ways than he would have liked to acknowledge. In addition to addiction to drink and, in his case, drugs, he was highly promiscuous and found it difficult to settle into domestic stability with anyone. True, he was with Frank Merlo for fourteen years, but this was an exception to the rule and an exception that was itself bedevilled by jealousy, rows and, frequently, sex with other men.

Again, like his father Tennessee lived much of his life on the move. Even though he was to own apartments in New Orleans (in the early 1960s he bought a house there, subdivided into apartments, in one of which he lived) and a house in Key West, which was the nearest he got to a permanent base, he too preferred to be away from home. Although Cornelius was a bully, the one wholly cruel action within the Williams family – Rose's lobotomy – was carried out at the insistence not of Cornelius but of Edwina. Social embarrassment at Rose's unladylike language and behaviour trumped any sense of maternal care or female solidarity.

If Tennessee's early emotional needs were met, to an unhealthy degree, by his mother rather than his distant and ungenerous father, it was his maternal grandparents, Walter and Rosina, who provided the calm and loving family setting essential to any child. Rosina, whom he called 'Grand', was from a German-American family. A talented musician, her piano lessons to paying customers were to be a useful source of financial support to her grandson in his student days. Their large rectory, which was reassuring proof

Tennessee Williams with his mother's parents, the Reverend Walter and Rosina Dakin. Williams was hugely fond of his maternal grandparents, and their home was a childhood refuge for him.

of social class for his mother, was to be a haven from his parents' unhappy marriage, while his grandfather's library was a source of joy. It was to be his grandfather who took the teenage Tennessee on his first trip to Europe, providing another major influence in his life.

The rectory was not just a respite on occasional visits, it was where he was to live for several years, including a twelve-month break from the unwelcome new surroundings of various unsatisfactory apartments in St Louis, the city to which his father moved the family for the sake of his career. Though Cornelius now had a management role with the excitingly named International Shoe Company, the nature of the work meant that he was living at home rather than travelling the country. This threw him and Edwina into closer proximity, with a disastrous effect on an already strained marriage. The children, inevitably, suffered emotionally from the tension between their parents. Though Tennessee's year with his Dakin grandparents was blissful, the downside was that when he was sent back, in order to give his sister Rose her own escape from their St Louis home, he found the return to urban life – and his father's unwelcome, boorish presence – almost unbearable.

In a professional life that was so strongly influenced by his private one, it is easy to see how Tennessee's idea of Blanche DuBois' family mansion, a Southern haven of gentility far removed from the working-class backstreets of New Orleans, originated. Belle Reve was a more glamorous, tragic version of his grandfather's Mississippi rectory – a place that had symbolized civilization, history and culture and which was now, itself, part of an irrecoverable past.

The role of nostalgia in Tennessee Williams's plays is one of the reasons for his popularity in England, a nation with a longing for a more glorious past at its very core. This takes many forms, from classically influenced modern architecture to television series such as *Downton Abbey* and *Wolf Hall*. In the Victorian era, artists like William Morris and the Pre-Raphaelites looked longingly over their shoulders to a pre-industrial England, while even in Tudor times there had been a harking back to the merrie England of the not-so-distant Middle Ages. Culturally, this makes Williams's dramas a perfect match for the English temperament, but his treatment of this yearning has, inevitably, a New World twist. The difference between the English and American approach to the same sense of loss can be seen in the contrast between Tennessee Williams and that of another great twentieth-century writer, the very English Evelyn Waugh.

Williams understood the appeal of the past. In *The Milk Train Doesn't Stop Here Anymore* he argues that 'Life is all memory, except for the one present moment that goes by so quickly you hardly catch it going.' Yet he showed the pity and the waste of living there: Waugh, by contrast, celebrated and championed it. The difference between them reflected an essential split between American and English culture in general – the Americans are almost as fascinated by the past as the English but, unlike them, are essentially more interested in the present and hopeful for the future.

Evelyn Waugh was a middle-class boy with an intense awareness of the minutiae of class distinctions. Though his father, Arthur, was a successful publisher and literary figure in his own right, he was not grand enough for his son. As a teenager, Evelyn would walk sufficiently far from his comfortable home in the unfashionable north London suburb of Golders Green to post letters in a postbox whose mail would receive the socially smarter distinction of a Hampstead postmark. A devout and rigidly conservative convert to Roman Catholicism, Waugh longed to be (or at least be taken to be) from a grand old Catholic family. His best-known novel, *Brideshead Revisited*, celebrated that class: titled aristocrats with country houses and private chapels. He wrote about such people and their way of life with a longing that gives the book much of its power, even though its central theme is ostensibly not class nostalgia but the spiritual journey of an atheist who comes to find God.

Williams, by contrast, though famous for his plays involving class – *The Glass Menagerie* and *A Streetcar Named Desire* in particular – and the inner conflicts of vastly wealthy families (*Cat on a Hot Tin Roof*), wrote about such people with sympathy for their predicament as individuals rather than in admiration of their social standing, let alone concern for their souls. Though he loved his grandfather, an Episcopalian priest, and was to convert, somewhat half-heartedly, to Catholicism in later life (pushed by his brother

Dakin, who had converted years before), religion was never the central force for Williams that it was for Waugh.

A further difference was in the surroundings that both men chose. Waugh's conversion to Roman Catholicism after his first wife left him (for an Old Etonian, which added to the humiliation he felt) was partly a desire to find something unshakable to hold onto in a rapidly changing world. He bought himself a country house, raised a large family and dressed like an old-fashioned country gentleman. Having satirized the English upper classes in his earliest novels, by his late thirties he had chosen to become a caricature of them.

The equivalent on the other side of the Atlantic would have been for Williams to buy a Southern plantation house and live there, surrounded by black servants, entertaining neighbours at sedate dinner parties and the occasional ball. Any such attempt to emulate the life of nineteenth-century Southern gentry would have been grotesque – and wholly out of character. Unlike Waugh, Williams was not a wannabe gentleman. He was, simply and wholeheartedly, a writer. His literary ambitions began early. Encouraged by his mother, who bought him a typewriter when he was twelve, he showed a precocious interest, earning five dollars, aged sixteen, for an article (published in *Smart Set* magazine) titled 'Can a Good Wife be a Good Sport?' – a piece that could, given his lack of sexual experience with women, let alone marriage, be classified as fiction rather than reportage.

In 1928 he had an Egyptian-themed horror story, 'The Vengeance of Nitocris', published in *Weird Tales*. The story showed an interest in Grand Guignol that was to be a feature of his mature writing. It also tapped into the fascination with all things ancient Egyptian that had been such a feature of Art Deco design and popular culture since the discovery of Tutankhamun's tomb by Lord Carnaervon and Howard Carter. That same year, Tennessee visited Europe with his grandfather. This was a major influence on him – a first, supervised, step towards the Continental lifestyle that he would enjoy as an adult, particularly in Italy. His grandfather's library had provided plenty of books about Greek and Roman myths and European culture. He had loved reading *The Iliad* and as a bed-bound child he had used the Jacks, Kings and Queens of playing cards to recreate the Trojan wars, casting them as gods and heroes. Now he was able to see Europe for himself, and the experience, a heady one for any seventeen-year-old, was to open him to a far older culture than that of his native America.

He wrote about several of the places he had visited for his school magazine. Though he clearly enjoyed Paris, London (viewed on the ground and then again in an exhilarating aeroplane tour from Croydon airport) and Monte Carlo, and though he dutifully visited an American war cemetery in northern France, his real enthusiasm was fired by Italy. His descriptions of Rome, Venice and Sorrento – including a hair-raising journey along hairpin roads, when the car he was in became locked in a dangerous duel with another vehicle, as each tried to block the other from overtaking – show a delight in the Italian landscape, climate and people that was to stay with him for the rest of his life.

Another enduring pleasure that he casually records in these teenage travel pieces was swimming. Whenever he gets the chance he takes to the water, and this was to be the one form of regular exercise that he enjoyed in a life otherwise unmarked by any interest in sport. He seemed to see swimming as a sort of amulet – a concession to the need to exercise and one that would surely provide the necessary protection against illness. Considering the way he poisoned his body with drugs and alcohol, this one nod to healthy living seems quixotic, but the regular, calming exercise may have had a real benefit after all, given that most men of his physical size would have succumbed to the pills and liquor decades before he did. As a young man, Tennessee swam at YMCAS – then, as he became more prosperous, in hotel pools and those of friends' villas – but on this formative trip to Europe he was plunging, whenever possible, into the Mediterranean.

Keen to become a writer, after leaving school Tennessee enrolled at the University of Missouri to study journalism. This was 1929, the year of the Wall Street Crash. He was not greatly interested in economics, which was too abstract a subject for him, but he did have an innate sympathy for and sensitivity to the plight of the many casualties of the Crash and the subsequent Depression, just as, later, he was to have for the European survivors of the Second World War in their poverty-stricken cities.

While at university, Tennessee began writing plays – two early ones were *Beauty Is the Word* (1930) and *Hot Milk at Three in the Morning* (1932). In the latter, he displayed his talent at creating striking titles, something he excelled at throughout his career. *Beauty Is the Word* is a one-act play involving an attack on puritanism, while *Hot Milk at Three in the Morning*, another short piece, was later adapted and turned into the one-act play *Moony's Kid Don't Cry*, published in 1941 and first performed in 1946. It expressed sympathy for the plight of the urban poor in America in the 1930s. The play wasn't long enough for much character development, but Williams's brushstrokes created a sympathetic central figure in Moony, a handsome, well-built young man (a recurring type throughout his work) whose marriage has gone wrong. Trapped in a poorly paid factory job, he longs for his earlier life as a woodsman in the countryside. Dissatisfied with his current life, he fondly remembers his father and the bond they used to have.

By contrast, the real-life relationship between father and son in the Williams household reached a new low when, in 1932, Tennessee was forced to leave university by Cornelius, who was unhappy at his son's lack of solid academic progress. Even though Tennessee's grandmother was supporting him with the proceeds of the piano lessons she gave young ladies, Cornelius insisted his son take a job. He paid for him to take a typing course (presumably for the

qualification rather than the skill, given the amount of time
Tennessee already spent at his own typewriter) and found him
a job at a St Louis shoe warehouse, owned by the company he himself
worked for. This job was a complete dead end, a frustrating and
humiliating experience that drove him to a nervous breakdown.
Williams tried to break the monotony by writing poetry on shoe
boxes (shades of the young Joe Orton defacing Islington library
books) and spending his evenings typing stories in his bedroom.
The time in the warehouse had some benefit, as he mixed with types
he would never otherwise have met, making him sympathetic to
working-class people in dull, repetitive jobs. Meanwhile, he had
the outlet, every evening, of losing himself in his writing – creating
at least one short story a week, crouched over his typewriter and
fuelled by black coffee.

His home life was mixed. Cornelius finally moved out, to Edwina
and the older children's relief. On the other hand, his sister Rose had
long been showing signs of mental instability. Tennessee was always
very close to her and found her psychological problems hugely
troubling. Due to his affection for her and his natural sympathy
for the underdog, he was understanding and supportive, difficult
though she could be. Occasionally, however, when exasperated by
her outbursts, he would snap, saying deliberately hurtful things.
These moments would haunt him in later life, when his sister was
a shell of her former self. Photos of Rose from this time show
a delicately pretty girl with an elfin face and gentle smile. Her
sweetness of character (albeit when not having one of her attacks
of hysteria) shines through, as it does in much later photographs,
as an old lady on outings with her famous brother. Looking at her
in these snapshots, it is easy to understand the protective devotion
that her brother showed her throughout his life.

Rose's psychological problems were, like so much around him,
a source of material for Tennessee's plays and she was clearly the model
for the character of Laura, the damaged young woman in his first

Rose Williams, Tennessee's sister, in her youth. Her mental illness haunted her brother, who feared that he might lose his own mind as well. His love and care for her, as soon as he could afford to support her, was lifelong, and she was the major beneficiary of his estate.

major success, *The Glass Menagerie*. She was also partly the inspiration for Blanche in *A Streetcar Named Desire*. In fact, there is a character called Rose in almost every one of his plays, as if every example of his art were in some way a tribute – or an apology – to her.

When Rose was lobotomized in 1943, after spending years in psychiatric units, he felt huge guilt that he had not been around to stop it. The trigger came when her hysteria (which emerged when she became sexually mature and which alternated with periods of intense withdrawal from the world) took the form of accusing her father of having a sexual interest in her. For Edwina, this was the final straw. It was not so much that she was determined to hush up a family secret (the reason for a threatened lobotomy in *Suddenly Last Summer*), but that she was not prepared to tolerate such a fundamentally unrespectable accusation. There is no way of telling whether Cornelius *had* behaved inappropriately towards his daughter, but given the way Rose used sexuality to shock her mother – on one occasion claiming to masturbate with church candles – this accusation of incest, with its subtext that if Edwina had been more receptive to her husband's sex drive he would not have developed ideas about his daughter, was perfectly calculated for maximum impact.

The lobotomy that Edwina decided to authorize was meant to cure patients of the worst aspects of a hysterical personality. The process, which involved slicing away part of the brain, was experimental and had obvious risks. In Rose's case the operation was something of a disaster: her personality was crushed and she was thereafter unable to live an independent life. From Edwina's point of view, however, the procedure was a success. There were no more accusations, no more hysteria and no more 'inappropriate' interest in sex. Rose's incarceration in a number of nursing homes kept her safely away from the neighbours. The terrible irony was that it was Edwina's belief that almost any interest in sex was revolting that had twisted Rose's own natural sex drive, leading to her various

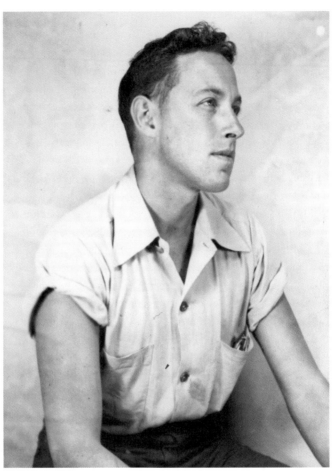

A dashing-looking young Tennessee Williams.

psychological problems. These problems profoundly affected Tennessee, who spent much of his adult life with the background fear that he would, like his sister, descend into some form of madness. As anyone who has seen *King Lear* will know, there is a special poignancy in someone who fears madness eventually succumbing to it. Williams used his family experience in his plays but its inclusion in his work never enabled him to exorcize fully the fear that his sister's illness, and the breakdown he had suffered at the shoe factory, would come back to claim him.

This was exacerbated by a lifelong guilt at not having been able to stop the operation going ahead. The drink and drugs that were, at least in part, taken as narcotics against these feelings, were, ironically, to heighten his natural tendency to nervous tension bordering on hysteria and helped push him into frequent states of mental collapse and, eventually, the spell in a mental hospital he so feared. After the lobotomy, Rose reverted to the personality and intellectual development of a child and was moved to a sanatorium. As soon as he could afford to help her financially, he did so, allocating to her some of his royalties and paying for her accommodation in a more comfortable nursing home for the rest of her life. He also, touchingly, had her come and stay with him for short periods, in a sort of holiday from institutional care, and would take her shopping, or out to restaurants, where she enjoyed ice cream, as most children do.

During Williams's early years he found refuge from family and drudge work not just in his writing but in trips to the cinema and to the theatre. Although he enjoyed seeing a range of American plays, including comedies and light dramas, it was a performance in 1934 of a European classic, Ibsen's *Ghosts*, starring Alla Nazimova, that sparked his desire to write for the stage. Twenty-seven years earlier, the same actress, starring in Ibsen's *Hedda Gabler*, had had a similar effect on Eugene O'Neill. She was clearly an inspirational performer.

The respite he received at his grandparents' house, where he recovered from the nervous breakdown at the factory, gave him the strength to co-write a short comedy about two sailors and their girls entitled *Cairo! Shanghai! Bombay!* with Dorothy Shapiro, a young neighbour of theirs. In his memoirs, after introducing Dorothy as 'very warmhearted and actively disposed', he ungallantly stresses that despite her getting star billing as writer, he actually wrote the play; she just produced the prologue. He goes on to describe her effort as 'undistinguished . . . Thank God the prologue was short: that's all I can remember in its favour.' He had happier memories of the audience's reaction to his work: 'the laughter, genuine and loud, at the comedy I had written enchanted me. Then and there the theatre and I found each other for better and for worse.' It was at this time that he also discovered the work of Chekhov, both as a playwright and author of short stories – the latter inspiring him to try harder at his own, winning a prize in a contest organized by the St Louis Writers Guild.

Having reacted so badly to the drudgery of life in an office, Tennessee was allowed to return to university, again supported by his grandmother. He briefly studied at the city's Washington University and had two plays staged by local amateur theatre companies – *The Magic Tower* and *Headlines*. The first was a one-act play about an artist and his actress lover whose tiny apartment is a refuge from the 'real' world, while *Headlines* was a very brief work (little more than ten minutes) on an anti-militarist theme.

Williams then moved (his student life proving as nomadic as his adult writer existence was to be) to the University of Iowa to study playwriting. Having left one form of madness, in the shape of Rose, at home, he encountered another at university. His course tutor, Professor Mabie, was a good teacher but suffered from a brain tumour, which made him mentally unstable, at times losing his temper with his students. The inherent problem this gave rise to was exacerbated by Mabie taking a strong dislike to Williams, based on the latter's camp mannerisms – even though Tennessee was gamely experimenting with straight sex at this point. Despite his tutor's lack of empathy, Williams enjoyed the course and finally emerged, in 1938, with a Bachelor's degree in English.

At 27, he was old for an undergraduate. He was also old for a virgin and was hugely pleased with himself when, at last, a fellow student – a girl with an impressive bosom and a taste for the bottle as well as for men – took care of this problem. Tennessee gave a graphic description of their lovemaking in his memoirs, though he did at least spare the girl's blushes by giving her a pseudonym. By this stage, he had had two more plays performed. *Candles to the Sun* was a full-length work set in a mining village and showed considerable empathy for contemporary social problems brought about by poverty and social and industrial unrest. Throughout his life he was to have sympathy for the underdog, though as has already been observed, his interest was in individuals rather than classes or socio-economic groups. If politics was referred to, or current affairs formed any sort of background to the events of the play, it was because they provided an interesting setting for the essentially private dramas of his characters. Though in the 1960s, when it was fashionable to do so, Williams claimed to hate rich people, he often enjoyed their company, if only because inclusion in their circle was a validation of his talent. Indeed, he was furious if he was left out of smart social gatherings that he felt he should have been invited to.

Candles to the Sun was staged by the Mummers, a St Louis theatre group with an interest in plays on social themes. *The Fugitive Kind* was a one-act play about love among the poor in unpleasant surroundings – a men's flophouse. Confusingly, the title was to be used, years later, in the film version of his play, *Orpheus Descending* – which was itself a remake of his play *Battle of Angels* of 1940. By the time he graduated, he had written two further plays – *Spring Storm* and *Not About Nightingales*. *Spring Storm* was unpublished and unperformed in his lifetime, receiving its first public outing as late as 1996, when it was given a staged reading in New York. Set in the South, in a small town on the Mississippi, it has as its central character a young woman called Heavenly – a name he would later use again in *Sweet Bird of Youth*. Though beautiful, she has ruined her chances of making a good marriage by losing her virginity – much to the horror of her socially ambitious mother.

Heavenly is proposed to by Dick, the appropriately named young man she has had sex with, but he has a low-level job and what Heavenly wants is a nice house and a well-brought-up family. This is offered by another suitor, Arthur, who unfortunately has to kill his existing girlfriend in order to free himself up to marry Heavenly. The fall-out from the death means he has to leave town, dashing Heavenly's hopes of a settled home – one for which she was even prepared to overlook her future husband's crime. In the end, therefore, she is left on the porch of her mother's house, without either man.

This play, though dealing with general themes of female sexuality and social respectability, along with the madness (and murder) that sexual passion can generate, is an entirely domestic drama, whereas *Not About Nightingales* was, like *Candles to the Sun*, inspired by contemporary social issues. The play is set in an island prison, where the inmates rebel against the brutal regime imposed on them by Boss Whalen, the warden. At the heart of the drama is a love story between a prisoner, Jim, and a prison secretary, Eva. It is unclear whether Jim, who flees the burning prison as police reinforcements arrive on the island, will make it to safety or not.

Written in 1938, *Not About Nightingales* was to have one production before being, in effect, forgotten until some sixty years later the radical English actress Vanessa Redgrave discovered the manuscript and was attracted to its strong social justice theme. The role of Boss Whalen was played by Redgrave's brother, Corin, an actor whose best work came in middle age, when he went from being the least known of Sir Michael Redgrave's children to a highly respected actor and box-office draw. The play was based on a real-life prison uprising, the Holmesburg Prison Strike, which took place the year the play was written. The strike ended with several prisoners being killed after being placed in a boiler room that generated an intense, unsurvivable heat. The play has a lot of short scenes, with intercuts, through lighting, between different locations in the prison, giving it a cinematic feel. The play itself may have been influenced by a penchant for prison dramas at the time.

Not About Nightingales may be the work of a young, inexperienced playwright, but it reads very powerfully. It contains some of Tennessee's trademark touches – violence, allusions to gay sex, the penalties of that sex (in this case syphilis), a camp gay character (Queen) and the way the spirit resists society's attempts to cage it. Tennessee felt sex should be a liberation: a natural need and a pleasure. In his own life and in the lives of his characters it was often far from ideal, and in *Not About Nightingales*, sex, like everything else in the prison, is cheap, furtive and fundamentally unpleasant. Talking with Eva of love, Jim says, 'Love is something nasty that's done in dark corners around this place.' The warden seems to have a 'normal' sex life – he has a wife and an infant daughter – but it turns out to be as sleazy and inherently violent as his regime of cruelty at the prison. We learn that his previous secretary, with whom he had an affair, died during an abortion.

Eva represents normality, youth and ideals. The warden tries to corrupt her too, and the playwright had enough maturity and knowledge of human nature to have her, despite herself, unwillingly respond when touched by him, even though her response, like the touch itself, disgusts her. Despite this, and her later offering of herself to the warden in order to save Jim, Eva represents decency and the outside world. The unofficial leader of the prisoners, Butch, despite his readiness to use violence, dreams (literally) of a normal life in the form of his ex-girlfriend, Goldie. He clings to the idea of resuming their relationship one day, even though she gave up writing to him ten years ago. Near the climax of the play, when between them Jim and Butch lead a prison revolt against the warden, it is of Goldie that Butch thinks as he goes to face the state troopers who have been summoned to put down the riot. It is his love for Goldie that humanizes him. Goldie is a brassier, less refined representation of femininity than Eva, but they are both female bringers of new life, their roles all the more appealing for the contrast to the sweaty, violently masculine setting. As such, they serve their purpose, but they lack the charisma and pathos of his later, iconic female roles.

While *Not About Nightingales* has poetry in it (literally, in the form of a quote from Keats, one of whose poems gives the play its title), as a play, it is distinguished from his later work by the overtly political message of the need for social reform and Williams's evident support for Roosevelt's government. Seeking support from the Works Progress Administration Writers' programme (part of the Roosevelt New Deal to get America back on its feet through government spending), Tennessee moved to New Orleans, which became, in effect, his spiritual home. He stayed, penniless, in a boarding house at 722 Toulouse Street. His experience here was the direct inspiration for his play *Vieux Carré*, of 1977, whose autobiographical central character is called, simply, the Writer. Williams not only modelled the Writer's rooming house on his own, he even gave it the same address.

New Orleans may have provided Williams with material, but New York was where any aspiring playwright wanted to be performed, so he was delighted when, in 1939, a collection of three of his one-act plays, under the umbrella title of *American Blues*, won a prize in the contest organized by the Group Theatre in New York City. The contest he had entered was for writers under 25, so he took three years off his age and signed the plays (accompanied by *Spring Storm* and *Not About Nightingales*) Tennessee Williams for the first time. He justified lying about his age on the grounds that he had lost three 'dead' years working at the International Shoe Company. The gesture has an air of gallant defiance about it, however self-serving.

The $100 prize also secured the support of Audrey Wood, a physically small but in every way redoubtable literary agent, who represented Williams for the next thirty years – until his increasing paranoia, fuelled by a lack of contemporary commercial success, led to a permanent rupture between the pair. The production of *Not About Nightingales* back in St Louis produced further financial help in the form of a $1,000 grant from the Rockefeller Foundation, and Tennessee, as he now was, seemed to have found the road to success. It was to be a longer, less linear path than he hoped. Though the money was welcome, it was not enough to completely change his circumstances. His nomadic lifestyle was still more a case of economic necessity than of intellectual curiosity, and he continued to take menial jobs to supplement the instalments of the grant that Audrey Wood forwarded to him.

Among the places he visited were California and, on the opposite coast, Provincetown, Massachusetts. The site, today, of an annual festival dedicated to his works, this was where he met and fell in love with Kip Kiernan, a Canadian dancer who left him for a woman and died young of a brain tumour, leaving memories that were, as so often with Tennessee, turned into a play script – *Something Cloudy, Something Clear*. The Provincetown Festival today plays an important part in promoting his work.

On 30 December 1940, Tennessee's full-length play *Battle of Angels* was performed in Boston, where it caused a storm of controversy due to its violence. The first major production of one of his plays, in a city he hoped would act as a springboard to take his work into New York and onto Broadway, turned out to be a disaster. *Battle of Angels* is set in a Southern town where a handsome young drifter, Val, on the run from a rape charge in Texas, arrives and causes a sexual maelstrom among the susceptible women – including Myra, the wife of the bedridden owner of the town's general store. The story, a take on the Orpheus legend, also has echoes of the life of Christ – an outsider murdered for his differences by the established authorities. This was made even clearer in its later incarnation as *Orpheus Descending*, where the action takes place over an Easter weekend. Such references were considered blasphemous in the 1940s.

The first night was a disaster, not least because during the dress rehearsal the scene where Myra's store is burned down after Val is killed with a blowtorch was something of a damp squib. The flame effects barely worked and the apologetic technical crew promised that on the night there would indeed be plenty of fire. Unfortunately, they seem to have overcompensated, and the audience (those who had not already walked out, as many did) were overwhelmed by huge clouds of smoke that suggested the fire might be at risk of spreading from the stage into the auditorium. In later works, Tennessee often preferred non-realistic sets and mere suggestions of buildings and effects, relying on the use of stage lighting and music to create a sense of place. Given what happened at *Battle of Angels*, this is unsurprising.

After the farcical events of the first night and the strength of the more generalized objection to the Boston opening – some people wanted the play taken off immediately on moral grounds – it was decided not to transfer to New York. Noël Coward's advice at times of crisis was always to 'sail away', and Tennessee, who sometimes did so literally on ocean liners, did the next best thing by heading for the coast, to Key West. The Florida Keys, a string of sun-drenched islands extending from the southern tip of Florida into the Caribbean, were one of his favourite places in the States. They were also to be the site of his home with Frank Merlo – but that relationship was still several years away at this point. In an ideal narrative he would have made a triumphant return to New York with a new play, typed on a table overlooking the ocean, but in real life he returned to a quasi-vagrant existence, taking another succession of short-lived jobs around the country.

While scraping a living this way he continued to write, working on short stories and one-act plays. Among these was *I Rise in Flame*,

Cried the Phoenix, a very short drama set in France, about the end of D. H. Lawrence's life. Williams was a great admirer of Lawrence's work, centred as it was on the primeval and primary importance of the sexual impulse in everyday life. The play has three characters: Lawrence, his German wife Frieda and a spinster English admirer, Bertha. The playwright's long-standing admiration of D. H. Lawrence had been sharpened in 1938 when he met Frieda in New Mexico. She was 59, with a heavy body topped by a shock of blonde hair looking, he felt, like a magnificent Valkyrie.

He began the play at the end, with Lawrence's death, refusing to be touched by the woman in his life. This was not from a lack of affection – the love between Lawrence and his wife is palpable in the dialogue – but because the manner of his death was the last area of life in which he could still exercise the masculinity that had defined his character and his prose. If Frieda was a Valkyrie, then Lawrence was an old-world warrior, determined to die as a man, raging against his imminent extinction.

I Rise in Flame, Cried the Phoenix, deals with Lawrence's belief that men have a fundamental need for women yet a simultaneous desire to be free of them. The paradox at the heart of this theory is that men (it claimed) require women for sex and to prove their masculinity, yet find the domesticity involved in making a home with a woman fundamentally emasculating. In what was to become a typical Williams touch of portraying women as birds, Lawrence frequently refers to his wife as a hen and claims to have a horror of the idea of women clustering round his deathbed: 'they'll moan and they'll flutter like doves around the burnt-out Phoenix – they'll cover my face and my hands with filmy kisses and little trickling tears . . .'

The poetry that was such a part of Tennessee Williams the writer was present in this very early work. Lawrence, in describing his longing to be well again and to return to the desert, where he can be fully male, in solitary communion with nature, says: 'I want to stand up on the Lobos and watch a rainstorm coming ten miles off like a silver-helmeted legion of marching giants.' Shortly afterwards, speaking of women and their ability to sense the approach of death, he claims, 'I think it's women that actually let death in, they whisper and beckon and slip it the dark latch-key from under their aprons . . .' Promising though all this was, Williams was capable of far better. At this early stage of his career, he was prepared to listen to others more experienced than he, so when Audrey Wood, who had taken him on as a client, persuaded him he could spend his time more profitably on other projects, he rounded the Lawrence work off and put it, like so many other ideas, in a drawer. *I Rise in Flame, Cried the Phoenix* was published in 1951, with an introduction by Frieda. It wasn't performed until 1959, when it was staged at the Theatre de Lys, where it had good reviews.

Lawrence also inspired one of Tennessee's poems. Although the imagery here too is of fire, it is of a different sort – the flame-red colouring of a fox. 'Cried the Fox', with its dedication 'For D.H.L', casts the red-haired writer as a wily force of nature and anticipates his inevitable death while celebrating his courage in refusing to be trapped or domesticated:

I run, cried the fox, in circles
narrower, narrower still,
across the desperate hollow,
skirting the frantic hill

and shall till my brush hangs burning
flame at the hunter's door
continue this fatal returning
to places that failed me before!

Then, with his heart breaking nearly,
the lonely, passionate bark

of the fugitive fox rang out clearly
as bells in the frosty dark,
across the desperate hollow,
skirting the frantic hill,
calling the pack to follow
a prey that escaped them still.

Though he was writing every day, Williams's itinerant casual jobs
continued for years. During this time America entered the Second
World War, following Japan's surprise attack on America's massive
naval base at Pearl Harbor in Hawaii in December 1941. Tennessee
wasn't called up, because he was physically unsuited to be a soldier.
This was not so much because of his size (Frank Merlo, his long-term
lover from 1947 onwards, was tiny – about 1.6 m/ 5 ft 3 in. – yet fought
bravely in the Pacific) but because of his eyesight – specifically, his
tendency to develop cataracts.

For some men this would have been a disappointment; for
Tennessee, it was a relief. As several entries in his journals make
clear, he was interested in the war only for its potential effect on
the theatre world: he admitted, for example, that the possibility
of the Theatre Guild discussing one of his plays was of far greater
importance to him than Germany's whirlwind invasion of Denmark.
Although when he wrote entries like this, he was being slightly
tongue in cheek – or, rather, aware of and amused by his own
selfishness – his attitude was shared by others across the Atlantic,
nearer to the action, whose lives were dedicated to the theatre above
all else. Shortly before the outbreak of war in Europe, in September
1939, John Gielgud, one of England's leading actors and a man
notoriously uninterested in anything apart from the stage, had
been weekending with friends in the country. He popped out to
the village shop to get a newspaper. On his return to the house
where the group were staying, his friends saw that he was ashen-
faced. They were horrified. Had war just been declared? 'Oh, I don't

know anything about that,' he replied, tears in his eyes. 'But I've just seen that Gladys Cooper has had the most awful reviews!'

Spared several years in the army, Williams carried on with a range of dead-end temporary jobs, on one occasion, while wearing a theatrically large pair of sunglasses during an afternoon off, being arrested as a suspected spy by a policeman who had clearly watched too many second-rate movies. His age and the fact that he was not in uniform further contributed to suspicions and he was held in a cell until he was able to prove that he was both an honest citizen and exempt from military service. It wasn't until 1943 that he was able to earn a living exclusively from his typewriter, when Audrey Wood negotiated a contract for the then considerable sum of $250 a week. When Williams first heard the figure, he assumed he was to be paid $250 *a month*. He was at that stage earning $17 a week as a cinema usher. This was fairly easy, low-pressure work that enabled him to see films for free if he wanted, and required no special training or skills. It also gave him plenty of time to people-watch. His time in this job was put to good use in the creation of two short stories and a one-act play. All are set in a cinema that was once an opera house. Such changes of use were not uncommon on either side of the Atlantic: for example, the London Coliseum, originally a theatre, was converted into a cinema for several years, before returning to theatrical use as an opera house, which it remains to this day.

The first story, *The Mysteries of the Joy Rio*, was written in 1941 but not published until 1954. In the story Pablo Gonzales (Tennessee using part of a lover's surname for the character), from Mexico, had been picked up as a young man by an overweight German watch-mender, Emiel Kroger, with whom he lived happily for many years. Now, long after Kroger's death, Pablo frequents an old opera house, the Joy Rio, currently used as a cinema, as his partner had done before him. Pablo is no longer young and Tennessee refers to the 'sweet bird of youth' having flown away from him. One day, during an excursion to the Joy Rio in search of sex, he falls foul of a (straight) seventeen-year-old usher, George, whose teenage girlfriend often comes into the cinema for illicit sex with him. Exhausted from climbing the stairs, Pablo stands on a landing, getting his breath back. Unfortunately, George thinks Pablo is some sort of voyeur, spying on him and his girlfriend. Indignant at this invasion of his privacy (albeit in a public lavatory, which is where the trysts take place), he attacks him. Pablo is saved by the manager but flees upstairs, where he is met by the ghost of his dead lover, who soothes and calms him as he dies from the stress of the situation.

The second story, *Hard Candy*, was also published in 1954 but was written only a year earlier. The central figure on this occasion is also gay and is in search of more tactile pleasure than any film projection can offer. Mr Krupper is a seventy-year-old ex-owner of a sweet shop, who finds sexual satisfaction in the upper reaches of the Joy Rio. One night he meets a beautiful young Latin American drifter and has sex with him, after offering the youth some of the sweets he habitually carries with him, as well as cash for sex.

Being fat and unattractive and perfectly aware of how repulsive people find him, Krupper has no problem with the financial aspect of the arrangement, especially when the lights come up for a minute between films, enabling the boy to see how unattractive he really is. Sex takes place and an overexcited Krupper has a heart attack. Rigor mortis leaves his body perched between two chairs, on his knees – where, it is implied, he was giving the youth oral sex. The presence of discarded sweet wrappers by the heart attack victim's body gives a newspaper reporter's coverage of the event a certain poignancy, given Krupper's previous occupation.

The first story is wistful, the second amusingly macabre, but both show, in their own way, their author's linking of sex and death. His play *These Are the Stairs You Gotta Watch* was first performed as recently as 2004, at the Kennedy Center in Washington. Also set at the Joy Rio, it has, like the stories, a description of the faded elegance of the building and the velvet rope that is used as a barrier between a lobby and the stairs leading to the upper reaches of the building. A new boy is inducted into the goings-on of the place and is warned (hence the title) how patrons like to get past the velvet rope barrier and up into the darker, unpatrolled parts of the cinema to have sex. He is shown the ropes, as it were, by Carl, who is 28, has a young family and is disgusted at himself for having worked as an usher for ten years. It is not, he feels, an appropriate job for anyone other than a teenager. This is a feeling shared by the playwright, who was beginning to despair of inappropriate jobs like these.

Mr Kroger is the unappealing manager of the cinema. Carl snaps when criticized by him, delivers a tirade of abuse – suggesting, in the course of it, that he was sexually interfered with by Mr Kroger years ago, when he applied for the post – and resigns. Not content with that, he goes upstairs to the locker room and sets fire to his uniform, which results in the police being called and Carl arrested. Meanwhile, a teenage girl, Gladys, tries to seduce the new usher, and the play ends with Gladys, having slipped under the rope, whispering urgently to him to join her, while the boy tries to maintain a professional focus on his new duties.

Happier things were on Tennessee's mind when he headed to California for his foray into Hollywood, for the MGM screenwriting job that Audrey Wood had secured for him. She had tapped into Hollywood's scattershot recruitment of any halfway decent stage writer or novelist to feed the demand for new scripts. This was still the Golden Age, when the cinema was king and needed a vast amount of product. He would now be writing for the movies rather than showing people to their seats while they played. Then, as now, the film world paid much better than theatre. The problem was that though it was lucrative, it was professionally frustrating. As a writer, Williams's ambitions remained firmly focused on a career in theatre. Like many of the other talented writers who went into the Hollywood system for money (including, bizarrely, the British composer, film star, West End matinee idol and playwright Ivor Novello, who in the early 1930s had a year in California, where he co-wrote the dialogue for *Tarzan the Ape Man*), he was frustrated at the nature of the films he was set to work on. Though he optimistically put a portrait of Chekhov on his office wall, the job he was given was as a vehicle for Lana Turner. Writing mindless dialogue for an actress he had little respect for – he was asked to keep to a minimum number of syllables in each word – was deeply frustrating, so he was relieved when the MGM management fired him before his six-month contract ran out, especially when he learned from Audrey Wood that though the studio had no further use for him, they were contractually obliged to keep paying him until the six months were over.

Financially, then, he had some leeway, but though he welcomed the money, what he wanted most was artistic recognition as a playwright. Theatre came to the rescue in the form of two productions – one in Cleveland, the other in California – of *You Touched Me!*, a play co-written with his friend Donald Windham, based on a D. H. Lawrence story. Having produced so much solo work without much success, Tennessee thought he may as well try a joint effort. *You Touched Me!* was the only example of a play by him that is set in England. A romantic piece about the adopted son of a country landowner who overcomes class prejudice (from his adoptive aunt) and wins the heart of his (adoptive, and therefore legally acceptable) sister, it deals, as with so much of the Williams oeuvre, with frustrated desire and people's need to break free from stultifying family ties.

The play won a cash award of $1,000 from the American Academy of Arts and Letters, money which helped fund him as he worked on a rewrite, for the theatre, of an unproduced screenplay he had been working on at MGM, *The Gentleman Caller*. MGM rejected it as a film project, yet it was with this, as a play and renamed *The Glass Menagerie*, that aged 33 Tennessee finally achieved the success that had so long eluded him.

The Donmar Warehouse (London) production of Tennessee's first hit, *The Glass Menagerie,* in 1995. Claire Skinner as Laura, with Zoe Wanamaker as Amanda.

2

The Later 1940s:
A Streetcar to Success

The Glass Menagerie is crucial to any study of Tennessee Williams's
writing. His first hit, it was one of the most profoundly autobiographical of his plays. It owed its successful transfer from Chicago to
Broadway, and then international fame, to the way it was nursed, in
its infancy, by theatre critics – a massive contrast to the way that, in
later years, other reviewers lined up to shoot down his newest plays.

The story involves a family, the Wingfields, whose father/husband
is absent. This absence is emphasized by a large photograph of him
as a young man, which hangs in the living room. The mother, Amanda,
is a faded Southern belle who resents being a middle-aged woman
living a dead-end life in a small apartment.

Her principal concern – and potential means of escape – is her
children, Tom (an obvious autobiographical touch) and Laura. Tom,
a writer, is also the narrator of the story. The daughter, based on
Rose Williams, is a damaged young woman who spends her time
obsessively organizing her collection of model animals – the glass
menagerie of the title of the play. Laura is a cripple, so her injury
is essentially a physical one, but the play makes it clear that she is
unworldly and sexually shy, which is why her mother is so desperate
to find a suitable young man to pair her off with. Left to her own
devices, her daughter would simply while away her time with her
collection of little glass animals. When, against the odds, Tom
brings home a work colleague, Amanda hopes that he might be the
'gentleman caller' she, if not her daughter, has been dreaming of.

The character of Tom is not only given Tennessee's original Christian name, he also, like the playwright, works in a shoe shop but has ambitions to be a poet. The name of the handsome workmate, Jim O'Connor, was that of a real-life friend of Tennessee's who was introduced to Rose in similar circumstances. The real Rose was ecstatic whenever Jim phoned, let alone called, and was crushed when, one day, he simply stopped doing so.

By 1944 Rose was not in a position to worry about being portrayed onstage, but Mrs Williams might well have done. However, she was delighted by the reviews and the resulting income and saw 'her' play several times. As a sign of gratitude for this reaction, in addition to any more general filial devotion, Tennessee signed over half the royalties to his mother, who was thus awarded a measure of financial freedom.

In the play it is discovered that Jim, who seems such good husband material and with whom Laura does indeed open up, is in fact so obviously a good catch that he has already been taken by another young woman, to whom he is engaged. This news is a terrible blow to Laura, who had begun to be drawn out of herself by Jim's good-natured and refreshingly straightforward attentions. Her reaction is, at once, to retreat into herself and focus on her glass menagerie – a focus that acts as a protective wall against the realities of the outside world and the adult life that she would be expected to live if she became a part of it. Amanda is devastated. Tom, the poet, leaves the defeated remnants of the family to cope as best they may, on their own – so they now have no male company or protection at all.

This made sense in the context of the play. Tom, the narrator, needs to make a life of his own rather than being trapped with two female dependants. His exit from the family home is also a reflection of how Williams left his own dysfunctional relatives behind in order to pursue his writing career. Its inclusion was a demonstration of the guilt he always felt about his sister's fate. That guilt may have been exacerbated by the fact that a year or two later (1946), he moved his by then widowed grandfather, the Reverend Walter Dakin, into his house in New Orleans. The retired priest had spent the previous five or so years living with his daughter, so Tennessee's offer of a home was in a way a second case of leaving the women in his family behind.

Tennessee's/Tom's guilt about Rose/Laura is made very plain in Tom's final monologue onstage, which also has a direct autobiographical reference to the playwright's hated factory work: 'Not long after that I was fired for writing a poem on the lid of a shoe box.' Tom then speaks of following in his father's footsteps by taking to the road, in a fruitless attempt to escape the memory of his sister and her silent torment:

> Then all at once my sister touches my shoulder. I turn around and look into her eyes. Oh, Laura, Laura, I tried to leave you behind me, but I am more faithful than I intended to be! I reach for a cigarette, I cross the street, I run into the movies or a bar, I buy a drink, I speak to the nearest stranger – anything that can blow your candles out!

It was not only the writing of *The Glass Menagerie* that had an impact, it was the presentation. For in his use of non-naturalistic sets, of music and light, of projections on screens to set the scene, and in the opening address of Tom to the audience, which included reference to the politics of the 1930s, the period during which the play is set, Tennessee showed himself not just to be a poetic writer but an innovator who had, with this play, announced the arrival of a new sort of theatre. His desire and ability to innovate, to present theatre in an unexpected way, was to earn him fame and financial success here, at the effective start of his career, but was, with a terrible irony, also to earn him the distaste and eventually the open hostility of theatre critics in the years to come.

At this point, however, reviewers played an entirely benevolent part in his life. *The Glass Menagerie* had, in the traditional way, opened out of town. The try-out, prior to the anticipated transfer to Broadway, was in Chicago, where the play opened the day after Christmas, on Boxing Day 1944. Opening so soon after Christmas might seem like commercial suicide, but Boxing Day has always been a prosperous one for the theatre, with families keen to get out of the house after 24 hours in the enforced company of close relatives. The drawback to the date is the likelihood of bad weather, and on this occasion Chicago lived up to its reputation as 'The Windy City'. There was an icy cold that was enough to put many people off leaving the warmth of their homes to see a new play by an unknown writer. The effect on box-office takings looked likely to bring *The Glass Menagerie* to a premature end, but two reviewers, Claudia Cassidy of the *Chicago Tribune* and Ashton Stevens of the *Chicago Herald-American*, not only gave it great reviews, but made several references to it in subsequent articles. This championing of the piece eventually had the desired effect, and enough people decided to give the new playwright a try. Word of mouth has always been the most effective promotional tool for any play and, given Williams's evident talent, the word worked and the transfer was assured.

It was not, however, enough to win the Pulitzer Prize for Drama, which in 1945 went to *Harvey*, Mary Chase's comedy about a giant invisible rabbit. Even at this stage in Williams's career, the establishment's judgement could be perverse.

The vital role of theatre critics in making or breaking a play was to continue throughout the twentieth century and into the Internet age. The most famous early example of this power occurred in London, in May 1956, when John Osborne's play *Look Back In Anger* opened at the Royal Court, in Sloane Square. The theatre critic Kenneth Tynan wrote in *The Observer* that he could not love someone who didn't admire the play. This was an astonishingly personal and vivid response to the work, triggered by the fact that the piece itself was so radical – it was the first of what were to be called 'kitchen sink' dramas, showing ordinary people in normal homes, instead of the parade of upper middle-class characters in grand drawing rooms with French windows that had been the main fare for contemporary plays until that point.

The Internet has radically changed all of this. Full-time theatre critics employed by newspapers are no longer the sole channel through which plays are brought to the attention of the general public, who can now read what numerous websites, blogs and social media accounts make of any given show. Major newspapers still influence their regular readers, but the magic circle has been blown wide open. Despite this, critics in New York – particularly those for the *New York Times* – still wield considerable power because, although the Internet offers an arguably more democratic approach to theatre reviewing, audiences often like to consult the experts before buying a ticket, especially when it comes to plays. At the time Williams was making his mark on Broadway, however, the critics' hold on the box office was unassailable.

What was then and is still the most important ingredient is naturally the play itself, so in the biography of a playwright their part in a success naturally takes precedence over any other, but for the general public the main attraction and most visible evidence of talent on any stage is the cast – specifically, the star. In *The Glass Menagerie*, this was Laurette Taylor, and the play was as much a triumphant return to form for her as it was a demonstration of Tennessee Williams's arrival, with a single leap, into the front rank of modern American dramatists. Taylor had once been a major star but the death of her husband, the playwright J. Hartley Manners, had sent her into an alcoholic spiral so disastrous that she had been banned from the stage by the actors' trade union Equity. She was, therefore, a courageous choice by co-directors Eddie Dowling, who also played the role of Tom, and Margo Jones.

The Glass Menagerie opened on Broadway at the Playhouse Theatre on 31 March 1945. Fortunately for the production, Miss

Taylor rose to the challenge, and, although she spent the press night being sick into strategically placed buckets in the wings when she wasn't needed onstage, she gave a radiant performance. She brought a sensitivity to the role of Amanda that astonished the playwright as much as it did the audience. She was less sensitive backstage, asking Edwina, when presented to her by Tennessee, 'Well, Mrs Williams, how did you like yourself?', before going on to explain that she had to arrange her hair differently to play the part, making herself look less intellectual than in real life, because the character was a fool!

Despite her lack of tact in the dressing room, she brought great artistry to the stage. The extra layer of meaning and emotion that a good actor, let alone a great one, can bring to the lines that a playwright has written can transform a part. An inflection in the voice, a look, a way of standing, a gesture, can add immeasurably in performance to the raw material that the performer has to work with. Even the author can be surprised at the power of his or her own words as revealed by an actor at this level. Laurette Taylor provided just such a gift in Chicago and then in New York, where the first-night reviews made it clear that Tennesee Williams had written a hit. The *New York Times*, then as now the most important review in town, praised the set and Paul Bowles's music, but, though it clearly liked the play (describing it as being as welcome as spring), it referred to flaws in the construction and dialogue and made it clear that the overriding reason it was recommending its readers to see it was Laurette Taylor's star performance. The triumph was, ultimately, Tennessee's, but it was Miss Taylor who had delivered it for him.

What attracted wartime audiences to the play, apart from the lead performance, the poetry of the language and the originality of presentation, was precisely that it wasn't about the war. We now know the conflict would be over in August of that year, but people were of course unaware of that at the time, and had it not been for the dropping of two atomic bombs, the conquest of Japan would have taken far longer. Military planners at the time estimated that victory would cost the lives of another million and a half Allied servicemen.

Theatregoers in wartime tend to prefer musicals, revues or light plays: one reason Noël Coward's *Blithe Spirit* of 1941 was such a hit in England was that, with its comic take on ghosts and mediums, it poked fun at death at a time when death was ever present in people's lives. Although reviewers picked up on the humour in *The Glass Menagerie*, it was, overall, a sad and wistful play. However, it was at least about families rather than war and had at its heart the concerns of peacetime characters. This helped make it something people wanted to see.

In 1947 Williams wrote an article called 'The Catastrophe of Success' for the *New York Times*, which was later reprinted in the Penguin Modern Classics edition, among others, of *The Glass Menagerie*. This was an essay on the changed circumstances that he now found himself in. In it, he says that he had not fully appreciated how much he had struggled through his twenties and early thirties – 'a life of clawing and scratching along a sheer surface and holding on tight with raw fingers to every inch of rock higher than the one caught hold of before . . .' – until the clawing mercifully came to a stop. The result, after the initial euphoria, was depression. To anyone who has not attained overnight stardom, this may seem a deeply ungrateful reaction, but it makes sense considering both his neurotic temperament and the nature of his approach to writing.

In the article, he claims that 'many people are not willing to believe that a playwright is interested in anything but popular success.' He certainly enjoyed the trappings, including a $125-dollar suit that he alludes to in the piece, but for him writing was far more than a way to make lots of money, however welcome. For him it was, as it had been since childhood, a means both of escaping unpleasant circumstances (no more menial, low-paid jobs) and of addressing the reality of the world around him – of rising above reality by taking his life experience and turning it, via his imagination and the dint of hard work and constant rewriting, into art. In the same article, he tries to describe how creativity is absolutely central to a writer's life:

> It is only in his work that an artist can find reality and satisfaction, for the actual world is less intense than the world of his invention and consequently his life, without recourse to violent disorder, does not seem very substantial. The right condition for him is that in which his work is not only convenient but unavoidable.

This was why he continued, for the rest of his life, to write. The money and the prestige created by each hit were by-products, making his new work all the more likely to be staged and for the wherewithal to lead his nomadic life in some comfort. All writers, whether of novels, plays or poetry, bring aspects of their own lives to the page, but this is particularly the case with Tennessee Williams. His life and art were inextricable, which is why when, some sixteen or so years after *The Glass Menagerie*, the critics began to turn on him, his offstage life went into a spin. As he came to depend increasingly on drugs and drink, his work also declined, in a vicious spiral. The criticism of his later plays – criticism that has become received wisdom – was wildly misplaced, for just as he brought a new sort of theatre to Broadway in 1945, so he did, or tried to do, in the 1960s, '70s and '80s, despite the odds that he had self-destructively lined up against his own success.

The sense of ennui, bordering on despair, that he fell into after *The Glass Menagerie* could only be cured by more writing and, in another example of behaviour that would be repeated through the rest of his life, through a change of scene. Now able to afford to travel in some style, he set out for somewhere completely different from Manhattan, choosing Mexico, where he enjoyed the sun, sea

and swimming, in an environment he was later to turn into a play
– *The Night of the Iguana*.

He also travelled to the Florida Keys, which just after the war
were relatively unspoilt and attracted an artistic community, as well
as fishermen and tourists. Tennessee liked the warmth and relative
informality – and the ready supply of sailors from nearby naval
bases. The combination of single men and sunshine, plus the
southern location far from the mainland, gave the place a raffish,
highly sexed atmosphere, though this was to turn sour many years
later, when his fame made him and the house he bought there a
target for occasional loutish and homophobic abuse. In the 1940s,
however, he was just another writer enjoying the sunshine and thus
relatively safe from unwanted attention. He spent the summer of
1946 in Nantucket, sharing a house with his friend the novelist
Carson McCullers. Then he returned to Key West, where he was
joined by his grateful grandfather.

His other companion was his first long-term partner, a young
Mexican, Pancho Rodriguez y Gonzalez. Handsome and well built,
Pancho had a mercurial temperament, setting the template for many
of the men Tennessee would be attracted to in later life. Tennessee
forgave Pancho the many scenes, including smashing crockery and
loud screaming matches, which punctuated their relationship. On
one occasion the director Elia Kazan physically had to bar the way
into his hotel room, where Tennessee, terrified, had fled from his
lover's latest violent rage. His letters to Pancho at such moments,
expressing love and concern, are touching proof of his devotion to
him. Even after they broke up and following Frank Merlo's arrival on
the scene, they stayed in touch. Tennessee's continued affection may
have been at least partly down to the value he had got from Pancho's
temper when creating one of his most memorable characters –
Stanley Kowalski.

The attraction had been (as with the brutish Stanley and his
higher-born wife, Stella) an essentially physical one. That much was

understandable to Williams's friends. What was less easy to see was why he put up with the rages and scenes that were an integral part of the relationship. The answer was that it was precisely this very Latin approach to love that Williams found so exciting – not least because it was the antithesis of the Protestant decorum his mother lived by. Pancho's aggression, Tennessee felt, was an expression both of his insecurity and of the depth of his emotional commitment to him. As someone plagued by a permanent doubt about his physical attractiveness, the devotion of a man so undeniably sexy was hugely welcome. In the end, however, it proved too disruptive. Work always came first, so the boyfriend had to go.

In September 1945 Tennessee's co-authored play *You Touched Me!* opened at the Booth Theatre in New York, directed by Margo Jones, the co-director of *The Glass Menagerie*. Despite starring a young Montgomery Clift, it was not a hit, not least because it suffered in comparison with the other, far stronger play. Tennessee's friendship with his co-author, Donald Windham, survived this setback, though it would eventually founder on a row over Windham's publication of Tennessee's letters to him.

During 1946 Tennessee worked on various small-scale projects, including *Ten Blocks on the Camino Real*, a surreal one-act play that was to form the basis of a later, full-length work, *Camino Real* (1953). He also wrote a short story, *Desire and the Black Masseur*. This was an example of his taste for the macabre and over-the-top, especially when it came to sexual desire. In a nutshell, the story is of a puny white man who enjoys being pummelled by a large black masseur who, realizing his client's taste for pain, gives him an increasingly brutal workout each time he visits. The contrast in race as well as size and sexual role gave an extra layer of transgression to the story, written at a time when racial segregation (in the South, at least) was part of everyday life. Eventually, after an almost pornographic descent into violence, both masseur and customer are expelled from the bath house when the client's scream of pain as his leg is broken is heard by the establishment's manager. The client is then killed and eaten at the masseur's home. Although it could be argued that the unspoken arrangement suited both men, even though it led to the client's death, *Desire and the Black Masseur* is at least superficially a far cry from Tennessee's other tales of doomed lovers or the need to follow one's sexuality to find real fulfilment. It does, however, tie in directly to the sense that runs through many of his plays (including *Orpheus Descending)* that sex is dangerous, with a real risk of violence and sudden, shocking death. Cannibalism, the most extreme coda to such an end, was also to feature in *Suddenly Last Summer*, when the offstage character Sebastian is beaten to death by a gang of adolescents who then start to devour his body.

The next year, 1947, was to be a crucial one for Williams's personal and professional life. For the latter, it was the year of *Summer and Smoke* and of *A Streetcar Named Desire*, both plays that dealt with frustrated sexuality. For the former, it was the year he met Frank Merlo.

For a man who wrote so often about frustrated sex lives, Tennessee Williams seems to have had a personal life that was the exact opposite. He had plenty of sex with Frank over the fourteen years of their relationship, as well as countless casual affairs, one-night stands and quick, sweaty encounters that did not involve an overnight stay. He wrote openly (some thought too openly for his own good) about this in his *Memoirs* of 1975. After getting over a couple of youthful infatuations with girls, Williams had cheerfully accepted his homosexuality and enjoyed exploring it with as many men as possible. Though not classically good-looking in a Gary Cooper or Montgomery Clift way, when young he had the allure of youth. He was also horny, confident and keen – all aphrodisiacs in themselves – and so had a high success rate. That he continued to be promiscuous during his relationship with Frank Merlo, to the extent that it eventually destroyed it, should not necessarily be a surprise.

Some relationships are not so much 'open' as yawning chasms, yet at the same time can be enduring, affectionate and mutually satisfying. If there was something slightly manic about Williams's philandering, it was in keeping with an addictive personality. It is an opinion rather than a judgement to suggest that there was something sad in his incessant search for sex, whether free or through paying rent boys. If it had made him happy, that would be one thing, but his memoirs suggest it was carried on through desperation rather than joy. John Lahr's magisterial biography of Tennessee, published in 2014, refers to this in the book's subtitle: *Mad Pilgrimage of the Flesh*.

Perhaps, like much of his writing, the accounts of Williams's affairs that appeared in his memoirs were an attempt to recapture, comment on or make sense of his earlier life. The frankness with which he recounted them, which many people found distasteful, was another case of his being ahead of his time. Alternatively, the graphic nature of the memoirs could be seen as part of a wider trend of self-destruction that finally saw him lose his life in yet another hotel room, in an accident involving a bottle of pills. That, however, was far in the future when, on 3 December 1947, the Barrymore Theatre hosted the Broadway opening of *A Streetcar Named Desire*.

This play, the best known of all his works and the one which seems to most define his writing style and character types, is set in a tenement building in New Orleans, where one of the well-born DuBois sisters, Stella, lives with her brutish but handsome, well-built and working-class husband, Stanley Kowalski. Into this small, crowded but essentially happy household comes Blanche, Stella's older sister, taking a streetcar named Desire to get to their apartment.

Often played by actresses in their forties, Blanche is actually meant to be thirty: a one-time society beauty whose looks have faded, in an era when a woman of that age was years past her sell-by date. The family home, Belle Reve (French for 'Happy Dream'), has

A photocall of the leading actors in the film version of *A Streetcar Named Desire*. Vivien Leigh (Blanche), Marlon Brando (Stanley), Kim Hunter (Stella) and Karl Malden (Mitch).

been 'lost', as it has been increasingly mortgaged to the hilt by a family whose physical decline – a string of deaths in recent years – matches that of their finances and status. Alone and homeless, Blanche has come to stay with her sister until something turns up. That something would, traditionally, be a husband. This was, after all, still a society in which a man was expected to provide the home, income and security without which any woman, regardless of her class, would be helplessly lost. The nearest potential suitor on offer is one of Stanley's card-playing friends, Mitch. Mitch is of a similar age to Blanche, not handsome but a decent man who has been emasculated by looking after his aged mother.

If Mitch is Blanche's safety net, then he is a distinctly second-rate one, but the possibility that he might catch her as she falls gives a dramatic tension to the scenes between them. The audience inevitably finds itself willing the couple on, even though the match would be an uneven one, with Mitch exchanging servitude to his mother with slavery to his wife. In the course of her stay at their apartment, Stanley comes to resent Blanche's airs and graces. He is also resentful of the loss of the DuBois fortune that he had expected partly to inherit through his wife. When he finds out that, despite presenting herself as the epitome of Southern good manners, Blanche has been reduced to earning a living as a prostitute, he passes the information on to Mitch, who declares his disgust for the woman he had hoped to marry. What upsets Mitch as much as Blanche's past is her hypocrisy. She has held out against granting him any sexual favours, despite their closeness, on the grounds that she is an old-fashioned Southern woman of good family who would not countenance sex before marriage. Her hopes of marriage are ruined, but her destruction is completed when Stanley rapes her. In the aftermath, she loses her mind, and Stella reluctantly has her committed to a mental asylum.

The play was an immediate hit, not least thanks to the inspired direction of Elia Kazan, whose wife, Molly Day Thacher, had been an early supporter of Tennessee's. Unlike *The Glass Menagerie*, critics and public alike loved the play from its first performance, transfixed by the sexuality, drama and – the playwright's trump card – the extraordinary poetry of his language. The combination of all three, along with brilliantly drawn characters, was powerful enough but was given a further emotional depth and tragic resonance by the intriguing, desperately sad back story of Blanche's husband. For it turns out that Blanche was not a spinster, but a widow. She had married a beautiful young man, Alan, when she, too, was very young. Her husband, who wrote poetry, turned out to be gay and was caught by Blanche in a compromising position with an older man. All three went out dancing as if nothing had happened but, unable to control her resentment, Blanche confronted him about his sexuality – 'You disgust me!' – on the dance floor. The boy, appalled that the one woman he thought might understand and somehow save him could reject him so callously, ran out and shot himself.

In some ways, Blanche's condemnation by Mitch is a mirror image of her treatment of her husband. Her guilt is something she always carries, and memories of Alan are triggered by the appearance of a young man collecting for charity, who comes to the apartment shortly before Mitch arrives, and who bears a striking resemblance – in Blanche's mind at least – to her dead husband. As she sees him, she hears the ghostly melody of a tune that was playing at the dance when the fatal scene took place. This use of music to add atmosphere or underline an emotion is characteristic of Williams's work. He had turned from poetry to the theatre as his main means of communication because the 'plastic' art of the stage – its three-dimensional living presence, its combination of words, movement and design – gave his ideas a greater life than printed words could, however haunting the mental images they created. It was this awareness of the potential for all aspects of stagecraft to work together for maximum impact that led to his frequent use of music, whether sung or instrumental, in his work. The guilt that the music triggers is similar to that which Tennessee felt about Rose: he had not been responsible for the lobotomy, but equally he had not been there to save her. He had been on the road, pursuing his dream of a writing career while Edwina blew out the candle that was Rose's tortured spirit. Blanche shares Rose's mental instability, while her promiscuity is what Edwina most feared in her daughter.

Sex, in the form of rape by Stanley, is what seals Blanche's fate, causing her to have a complete breakdown. She has to go to the asylum because Stella cannot continue to live with Stanley if she believes Blanche's accusations. Rather as male lions kill the previous cubs of lionesses they find and mate with to ensure the primacy of their own gene pool, so Stanley destroys his wife's only remaining relative while she, Stella, is in hospital having his baby. There is to be no challenge to him within the family now he has a child. He is fulfilling his alpha male role in as primitive a way as a wild beast.

Though it is Stanley who destroys Blanche, Williams, with his inherent distrust of family relationships, based on his own experience, blames the DuBois family, in its decadence, promiscuity and profligacy, for driving her out of Belle Reve and into the Kowalski family apartment in the French quarter. Defensively telling Stella how Belle Reve came to be lost, Blanche describes the pressures she was under as the family disintegrated, through illness and debt, around her: 'I, I, I took the blows . . . All those deaths! The long parade to the graveyard! Father, mother! Margaret, that dreadful way! . . . How in hell do you think all that sickness and dying was paid for?'

The play's most famous line – 'I have always depended on the kindness of strangers' – is not just an example of Blanche's clinging to the shreds of dignity and good manners in the face of tragedy. It is an indictment of the lifelong failure of her family: she has always *had* to depend on strangers because her family have proved wholly incapable of giving her the support, shelter or kindness she needs. Whoever is at fault, their failure has led Blanche into Stanley's clutches. Her fate is sealed by his brutishness, which she finds repellent: 'Deliberate cruelty is not forgivable. It is the one unforgivable thing in my opinion and it is the one thing of which I have never, never been guilty.' As with any tragedy, however, the central protagonist is herself partly to blame, for she flaunts her sexuality, completely inappropriately, in front of Stanley from the moment they meet. Early in the play she says, lightly, to Stella, 'I was flirting with your husband, Stella!' Just before he rapes her, Stanley insists, 'We've had this date with each other since the beginning!' In the production of *A Streetcar Named Desire*, at London's Young Vic theatre in 2014, Gillian Anderson brilliantly caught this fundamentally self-destructive behaviour.

Anderson is one of the most recent in a long line to have played Blanche DuBois. It is one of the great female roles in Western theatre and has been performed by generations of remarkable actresses. These include Cate Blanchett, who also won the Oscar for Best Actress in 2014 in the title role in Woody Allen's film *Blue Jasmine*, the initial scene of which has echoes of *A Streetcar Named Desire*: a once wealthy woman, suffering from mental health issues, comes to stay with her sister and her working-class lover in a working-class neighbourhood. The first Blanche, at the New York opening in 1947, was Jessica Tandy, who won rave reviews and a Tony Award for her performance. These days she is probably best remembered, in old age, for the film *Driving Miss Daisy*, playing a very different – and vastly older – Southern lady. Although Tandy created the part of Blanche and was wonderful in it, the performance against which all others are inevitably measured is that of Vivien Leigh, who was immortalized in the film version.

Vivien Leigh (1913–1967) first played Blanche in London in 1949, in a production directed by her husband, Sir Laurence Olivier, at the Aldwych Theatre in London. At the time, they were the golden couple of British theatre, and were treated like royalty when they went on overseas tours. Leigh reprised the role on film in 1951, winning the Oscar for Best Actress the following year – accompanied by Kim Hunter, reprising her Broadway role as Stella, and Karl Malden as Mitch, who both won Oscars in the Best Supporting Actress/Actor categories. Acting is a notoriously back-stabbing business, but Olivier's reputed reaction to his wife winning an Oscar when he had not (he wouldn't speak to her in the limousine on the way back to their hotel) is one of the more striking examples of professional jealousy overcoming the normal ties of spousal affection.

Leigh, a stunning beauty when young, was a great actress, very highly sexed – Olivier, who eventually divorced her in 1960, complained she was a nymphomaniac who would not let him get the rest he needed after a performance – and suffered from bouts of mental illness. She would later claim that playing Blanche tipped her into madness, and she brought the fragility of her own personality to the role with spectacular effect. Because of the long love affair between London audiences and Tennessee Williams's plays, it seems curiously fitting that his greatest role should be best known through the interpretation of an English actress. Given the power of the story and her skill as an actress, it is not surprising that her screen role was so memorable, but what gave her performance even greater impact was the chemistry between her Blanche and Marlon Brando's Stanley Kowalski.

Brando was a strikingly attractive unknown young actor when he read for the part of Stanley. To do so, he visited the writer and others associated with the production when they were staying at a small cottage on the coast, at Provincetown. Brando, who arrived with a beautiful young woman in tow, took method acting to new heights when, on being told that the house's lavatory was blocked and electrics malfunctioning, sorted both out with his bare hands. He then gave a superb reading but, thanks to the unblocking, the restoration of light, his muscles and his charm, the part was already his for the asking.

A Streetcar Named Desire was directed by Elia Kazan, who would also direct the screen version. He and Williams, who had the greatest respect for each other, would also work on *Baby Doll*, the controversial film of 1956 based on an amalgam of three of Williams's short stories. In a letter to Hollywood's censorship body, the Production Code Administration, Tennessee defended *A Streetcar Named Desire*'s translation into film on the grounds that, far from being a salacious shocker, it was a lament for 'the ravishment of the tender, the sensitive . . . the savage and brutal forces of modern society'. Blanche, with her love of poetry, her longing for a gentler, more civilized past, represented the sensitive, while Stanley was the embodiment of the tough, industrialized, post-war world. Stanley is not entirely unsympathetic. Obviously his brutality, particularly when it culminates in the rape of his sister-in-law, is entirely reprehensible, but what he does offer is evidence of the energy, physical strength and determination of the modern age. He is of his time; he is in charge of his fate. He may be a thug but he is not a victim. In a way, he is indicative not just of every new generation of immigrants to America, with their determination to succeed, but of the first Europeans, the pioneers, who metaphorically raped the countryside and trampled on the indigenous culture in order to hack out their own share of the American Dream. The play suggests that the modern dream is, in fact, a nightmare, and that grace and poetry are irrevocably part of the past. Dreaming of them, then, is an entirely unproductive, backward-looking and enervating activity that can bring nothing but tears. The playwright argues this not as one who is dismissive of the past, but as one who desperately regrets its passing. This makes Blanche's situation, her self-destructive inability to adapt to the modern world, all the more moving.

Tennessee was always nostalgic for the grace of the Old South, grace that still rippled in people like his grandmother and in places, like parts of New Orleans, that he knew well. *Streetcar* managed to combine the contrast between the poetic and the brutal with a cross-section of everyday life (the Kowalski's neighbours, for example), yet alongside the representation of this there ran through the piece an almost operatic sense of heightened tension. All these factors blended in a uniquely powerful new drama. That newness should not be forgotten. More than 65 years after it was first performed, and considering its place in the canon of Western drama, it is easy (and usual) for *A Streetcar Named Desire* to be seen as a classical play – in marked contrast to Tennessee's far more experimental work of the 1960s and 1970s. However, the mixture of poetry and sex that the playwright brought to the stage was new, different and dazzling. On the other side of the Atlantic, in England, Christopher Fry would lead a short-lived trend for verse plays on the London stage, but, mesmerizing though his work could be, it lacked the extraordinary dramatic power, the dangerous sexuality, the aching sense of loss that Tennessee brought to *A Streetcar Named Desire.*

The downside of writing a masterpiece is that it is a very hard act to follow, and so it proved with his next Broadway opening, *Summer and Smoke*. First staged in Texas in July 1947, it was meant to move straight to Broadway but was delayed for the opening of *Streetcar* and only joined it in New York in October 1948. It closed in January the following year, yet was to prove a much-loved play in subsequent productions, one of the most notable of which was José Quintero's, in 1952. Starring Geraldine Page, this established the piece as a major work.

Like *A Streetcar Named Desire*, *Summer and Smoke* also has a damaged female as its central character. In this play, however, it is her lack of sexual experience, rather than a surfeit of it, that is the problem. The central relationship is between Alma Winemiller, an attractive young woman, and John Buchanan, a young man about town and the son of the respected local doctor. Alma believes that love is all about the soul, while John is more interested in the body – at one point he makes Alma look at an anatomy chart, to illustrate that people are physical creatures – with physical needs that have to be recognized and satisfied. Alma sings beautifully – a representation of the purity of her mind. Her tragedy is that she cannot unbend enough to make love to the man she has loved all her life (they are first seen in an opening prologue with the two of them as children), but whose unashamed sexuality unnerves her. In the course of the play, their roles reverse as he, following a family tragedy, pulls himself together and takes over his father's role as the local doctor (symbolic of respectability) and marries a nice local girl. Alma, by contrast, having left it too late to marry John, has now gone to the other extreme and accompanies strangers to the local Moon Lake Casino, where, it is implied, she has sex with them in the grounds.

Summer and Smoke argues the case against puritan sanctimoniousness about the physical expression of love and for the realization that humans are sexual creatures. In some ways, Alma is based on Tennessee's mother, Edwina, whose own puritanism wrecked her marriage to Cornelius. Her warped view of sex affected Tennessee as a young man: he claimed to have been so hung up about his body that, although he had wet dreams and spontaneous orgasms when touched by someone he found attractive, he didn't masturbate until he was 26. Not surprisingly, he went rather overboard in making up for lost time. Alma's fate is far less dramatic in this story than Blanche's, but it is still a sad one; another woman whose life has taken a wrong turn and will continue downwards, any hope of redemption or fulfilment getting daily further out of reach. The disappointing reviews for *Summer and Smoke* made unflattering comparisons to *A Streetcar Named Desire*. This was largely a question of unlucky timing. Had the plays been produced in New York the other way round, then *Summer and Smoke* would undoubtedly have fared far better. As it was, Williams decided to put some physical and emotional distance between him and Broadway by travelling to Italy.

He had liked Europe on his visit with his grandfather in 1928. He was attracted to its way of life, if not its politics. Once he had embraced the fact that he was gay, he found the European attitude towards sexuality, despite the influence of the Roman Catholic Church, to be far more liberal, in practice, than that in the United States. Specifically, it was Italy – an older south than that of the States, but one with corresponding sun and sensuality – that took such a relaxed view. Besides, who would not be attracted to Italians? Another fundamental attraction for him was Europe's cultural heritage, particularly that of the classical world. Though he enjoyed France, which since the 1920s had been a magnet for expatriate American writers, Italy had a greater concentration of the factors that drew him to the Continent and provided a direct link to classical civilization.

On his first trip he had been financially dependent on his grandfather. Now he had money to spend and time to spend it. In 1928 the country had seemed, for better or worse, to be part of the future, with the groundbreaking Fascist government of Benito Mussolini. As Muriel Spark's novel *The Prime of Miss Jean Brodie* made clear, for many people in Western Europe, Mussolini represented modernity allied to a brutal glamour. This admiration was heavily influenced by the classical education that was still the basis of British upper-class schooling. Mussolini self-consciously adopted the mantle (however ill-fitting) of ancient Rome, putting maps of the old empire on walls in modern Rome while he tried to emulate the caesars by adding to Italy's existing empire (Libya) with the controversial conquest of Abyssinia (modern-day Ethiopia) in 1936. Now, after the war, Mussolini and his regime were just a bad memory. Whatever appeal he once had was buried by his having led the nation into a disastrous war in which Italy was hammered not only by the British and the Americans but by the Germans who were originally their allies but became, on Mussolini's dramatic overthrow by the King of Italy in 1943, their occupiers and persecutors.

In the immediate post-war era, Italy, far from being a country noted for its modern, though controversial, politics and for its renewed sense of destiny, was a bankrupt nation on the losing side of a devastating war. It had to rely on its climate, history and natural beauty to attract tourists – and their desperately needed cash. Visitors may have considered 'O Sole Mio' to be the national song, but an equally appropriate – and darker – number would have been Cole Porter's hit of 1930, 'Love For Sale'. Young women and, more to the point here, young men, were willing to swap sex for dollars. For

Tennessee at the Memorial Service for Dylan Thomas in New York, after the latter's early death in 1953.

Tennessee, this combination of youth, beauty and availability was entrancing – and not just for him. His new friend Gore Vidal, author of a groundbreaking gay novel, *The City and the Pillar*, joined him for an Italian holiday in 1948, attracted by the present-day sexual opportunities as much as his genuine fascination with Rome's imperial past. They had in fact met in Rome, where Americans were discovering attractions that, before the war, had been traditionally enjoyed by English expatriates.

The two men hit it off immediately, in an attraction of like minds – both being gay, creative and keen for experience to translate into art. In this respect, Vidal had much in common with many of the friends that Williams made during his life: attractive and artistic. Williams numbered poets, painters, writers, sculptors and dancers among his circle. Especially as a young man he found the aura of emerging talent, in whatever field, hugely attractive. Physically, the two new friends were a considerable contrast – Vidal tall, slim, elegant and aristocratic; Williams short, stocky and Bohemian. Williams was also a decade and a half older and so, in effect, a generation above Vidal, to whom success, or at least fame, had come far earlier. Another contrast was that Vidal had served during the war and was fascinated by politics – later running for Congress and moving, thanks to being related to Jackie Kennedy, in the highest Washington circles. What they had in common, apart for a taste for drink and literature, was an attraction to young men and a determination to enjoy the freedoms offered by post-war opportunities for travel.

Arriving initially in Paris, Tennessee checked into the George V, arguably the city's grandest hotel. Greta Garbo had recommended it to him, but he found it soulless. Alone, unhappy and disliking the food, he drank too much and ended up at the American hospital at Neuilly. Here he was rescued by Madame Lazareff, the editor of *Elle*, the fashion magazine, whose daughter he had befriended on the voyage across the Atlantic. Insisting he come to her house to be properly fed and rested, his rescuer suggested the best thing he could do, once he recovered, was to head for the sunshine of the South of France. Taking her advice, he travelled to Vence. Perhaps it was the town's association with death – D. H. Lawrence had died here – that made Tennessee find it and the white doves that fluttered around like so many lost souls deeply depressing, so he moved forwards (*En Avant!* as he liked to say) to Italy. In his memoirs he wrote that as soon as he crossed the Italian border, his health was restored: 'There was the sun and there were the smiling Italians.'

Among them were the film director Luchino Visconti and his assistant – and lover – Franco Zeffirelli. Williams found nothing disconcerting about the evident clash between Visconti's Communist politics and the fact that he was an aristocrat with money, white-gloved servants and a luxurious lifestyle. On the contrary, he thought that, except in the case of Bertolt Brecht, an artist's politics had little influence on his work, or, rather, on its value. What mattered was his talent and, above all, his humanity. Zeffirelli was later to be one of the great figures of twentieth-century Italian cinema and opera. Intrigued though he was by Visconti and his circle, Williams's greatest interest was in humbler – and more available – Italian men. The United States dollar was at an all-time high against the lira, giving ample opportunity for an American visitor to enjoy the benefits of a full wallet. This situation was to be the inspiration for his novella *The Roman Spring of Mrs Stone*, published in 1950, as a new decade began.

3

The 1950s: A Cat on a Hot Tin Roof

For Tennessee Williams the 1950s began with a book rather than a
play – a sign of the range of his talent and his desire to experiment.
Though the result was one of his most impressive pieces of writing,
it would be a quarter of a century before he produced another – the
almost unreadable *Moise and the World of Reason.* With its wholly
bizarre plot, this would prove as much a failure (and for better
reasons) as his plays of the same period. In *The Roman Spring of
Mrs Stone*, however, he created a small masterpiece. It seems to be
little known today, which is curious because quite apart from the
extraordinary quality of the writing, it deals with Tennessee's themes
of losing one's youth and beauty and the imbalances and indignities
that go with sexual relations between the wealthy middle-aged and
the attractive but poor young. It also gives a memorable, astutely
drawn picture of a leading stage actress and the world she inhabits.

As it was his first novel – although technically, at just over a
hundred pages, a novella – and therefore in a very different medium
from the one he was used to, one might expect it to show signs of his
inexperience with the genre. In fact, it reads incredibly well and the
art form enables him to describe rather than show – as onstage –
the psychology of the principal characters. These include Karen
Stone, Paolo de Leon, The Contessa and an unnamed youth who
is, in effect, stalking Karen.

Karen is a middle-aged American actress, once a great beauty
but now very aware that she has lost the looks that brought her the

leading roles that made her a star – in an age when an individual could still be a 'star' without leaving the stage for the screen. When the novel begins, Karen is living in Rome, after having suffered three great losses. The first was her looks, which have been replaced by a certain grandeur:

> The knowledge that her beauty was lost had come upon her recently and it was still occasionally forgotten . . . It could be forgotten sometimes in the company of Italians who had never seen her as other than she was now . . . But Mrs Stone had instinctively avoided contact with women she had known in America, whose eyes, if not their tongues, were inclined to uncomfortable candour.

The second loss, following on the first, was of her stage career, from which she retired after an ill-advised decision to play Juliet when she was far too old for the role. (Ironically, in the ballet world, Juliet is generally best danced by ballerinas in the later stages of their careers, when they can bring an emotional maturity and acting experience to the role, while their slimness enables them still to look the part onstage.) The third blow was the death, while on the world tour that immediately followed her retirement, of her husband, Tom Stone. A small, dumpy man, he had been her greatest supporter and, conveniently, was enormously rich. His death from a heart attack left her a very wealthy widow but bereft. Their relationship had been sexless but what could have destroyed it was in the end the making of it:

> Their marriage, in its beginning, had come very close to disaster because of a sexual coldness, amounting to aversion, on her part, and a sexual awkwardness, amounting to impotence, on his. If one night, twenty-five years ago, he had not broken down and wept on her breast like a baby, and in this way transferred his

position from that of unsuccessful master to that of pathetic
dependent, the marriage would have cracked up. But the pathos
had succeeded where desire had not. She had taken him into
her arms with a sudden tenderness and the marriage had then
suddenly been set right, or at least been salvaged. Through his
inadequacy Mr Stone had allowed them both to discover what
both really wanted, she an adult child and he a living and young
and adorable mother.

Choosing to stay in Rome rather than return to the States, she
falls in with an impoverished contessa who earns a living pimping
out beautiful but poor young men, often from good families. The
tension inherent in the boys' situation is exacerbated by their
awareness of their good breeding, even while they pay court to
women who are not only far older than they are but representative
of a modern age which has no place for their family trees and coats
of arms – a metaphor for the radically changed balance of power
between the United States and Europe in the post-war world.

The book is a reminder not only of this shift in power, but of the
everyday presence of poverty and hunger, which gives a dimension
of urgency and need to the various relationships. The nameless
young man who stands at the foot of the Spanish Steps, gazing up at
Karen's apartment, is very attractive – 'His beauty was noticeable
even in a province where the lack of it is more exceptional in a young
man' – but is desperately poor:

> his mouth tightened with discomfort, and secretly, fearful
> of betraying a thing so shameful, his long cold fingers crept
> inside his black overcoat and pressed themselves against the
> warm, aching centre of his body where hunger was and had
> been for many days and nights past since he had descended
> from the shell of a town among the hills south of Rome . . .

This poverty, which reflected the reality of the post-war Rome that Tennessee stayed in, makes commercial sex a part of everyday life – not just in red light districts, but in well-known and popularly frequented places like the Spanish Steps. As he keeps his lonely vigil, the boy is accosted, politely but unmistakably, by a male American tourist who has stopped near him and reached inside his jacket to bring out a packet of cigarettes: 'If accepted, that offer would have a sequence of others, dispelling hunger and every other discomfort for days to come.'

While the young man hopes Karen will notice him, she has eyes only for Paolo, aristocratic, in his early twenties and the most handsome – and narcissistic – of the contessa's stable of young men. Williams describes his looks: 'Paolo's young skin was flawless. It was the colour of very rich creams and almost as fine to the touch.' But the author's real skill is his description of the boy's character and his petulant – and sometimes comical – way of speaking to Mrs Stone, especially when, once their affair finally begins, they argue.

Used to finding rich 'protectors' for whom he has nothing but contempt, he realizes there is something more to Karen Stone – apart from being richer than his other, male and female, patrons:

> Paolo was too much the vain young dandy of the world to see or want to see much beneath the surface of a nature more complex than his . . . And yet even Paolo, with his minimal perception, had noted in Mrs Stone the existence of a certain loneliness, unusual in kind as well as in degree, which a young adventurer no more encumbered by scruples than himself could turn to his great advantage once he got past her little walls and defences.

Those walls and defences last longer than either Paolo or the contessa expect, because Karen Stone has further to fall than most rich Americans visiting the Eternal City:

Mrs Stone knew, as well as Paolo knew it, that to become the aggressor in a relationship is to forsake an advantage. She, too, had once held the trump card of beauty which he was now holding and she had held it for such a long time that, although she now admitted to herself in private moments of candour that it was no longer hers, her social manner and procedure were still based upon its possession. She showed as plainly as Paolo that she was more used to receive than to offer courtship.

Lonely and with a new-found physical desire partly released by the immunity from unwanted pregnancy that the menopause has brought, Karen allows herself to fall for Paolo, and makes the mistake, despite her awareness of the financial subtext, of hoping that there is a genuine romance involved, too. With this surrender of aloofness goes the inevitable – given the age difference and her lover's total self-absorption –– loss of dignity. Humiliated by his flirtation, in front of her, with a young woman at a society dinner, she tearfully remonstrates with him in the back of her chauffeur-driven limousine, insisting that she is not like his other conquests and should be treated accordingly, even though she knows, as she does so, that she has sacrificed any shred of self-respect by pleading with him this way: 'So it had happened. It had been lost, all dignity, and now she was frantically digging a handkerchief and a compact out of her bag while her breath came in sobs.'

Dismissive of her distress, he turns the attention back to where he prefers it – himself – in a ludicrously self-regarding attempt to suggest that he, too, is a person of some standing in the world: 'Let me remind you that I have been photographed too. . . . And you are not the first great lady I have been out with.'

As they arrive at the gates of the palazzo where she has her apartment, Karen, now calmer, says, 'You are right, Paolo . . . it is not a dignified subject, and I think the worst thing about love between a very young and a somewhat older person is the terrifying loss of dignity that it seems to call for . . .'

That evening the affair ends as Paolo moves on from Karen to a young Hollywood starlet visiting the city. Desperate, with her loneliness all the greater and the vast white expanse of her empty bed mocking her as she stands in the palazzo, completely alone and with her reputation in tatters, Karen grasps at the dangerous opportunity represented by the beautiful stalker. Previously disturbed by him, as he trailed her round the streets of Rome, she now sees him as a way out of her isolation – and a solution to the insistency of the sexual desire that her affair with Paolo has brought to vivid and sometimes overwhelming life.

Vivien Leigh, the very English actress and beauty whose most famous screen performances were as American women fallen on hard times – Scarlett O'Hara in *Gone With The Wind* and Blanche DuBois in *A Streetcar Named Desire*. She is seen here in her third (though barely known) great American role, Karen Stone, opposite Warren Beatty as a young Italian aristocrat (and gigolo) in the film of Tennessee's novella *The Roman Spring of Mrs Stone*.

She knows she cannot tolerate what she calls 'the drift' – the aimlessness of life as a rich foreign widow in the heart of Italy: 'The drifting that was nothingness went on. Something, she said to herself. Anything at all, except nothing. Nothing could not be allowed to go on and on and on like this!' Her decision, when she throws the keys from her balcony to the waiting boy below, is a potentially fatal one. The boy represents a common theme in Tennessee's plays and stories – the link between desire and death. However, Mrs Stone doesn't care about the risks attached to letting the boy into her apartment. She wants to end the drift that characterizes her life and if that means a violent death, then so be it.

The Roman Spring of Mrs Stone has a simple but gripping plot and, as discussed, looks in detail at the typical Tennessee concerns about age, sex and money. There is another aspect that makes it fascinating for today's readers, if they know his plays. For his description of the life of a leading actress, a national figure, gives an insight into how a star of the late 1940s and early 1950s would live. Although in practice it satirizes such people, the book rings true about a heartlessly efficient way of life, in a milieu where, apart from her husband, the theatre community is the only family she has. Williams shows her to be essentially heartless – her visits to sick members of the company, the blizzard of birthday cards her secretary religiously sends out, the flowers sent for every occasion from birthdays and weddings to funerals: all these are things she does because a star is supposed to, not because she cares at all for their recipients. Her career is everything to her, while at the same time, despite her almost photographic memory for learning lines and her skilful use of stage technique, her position in the theatre world is based not on her acting ability but on her remarkable beauty.

The contrast between her previous, pre-widowhood life and her new, drifting existence in Rome is very powerful. We learn that the one time she had sex with one of her leading men was an act of aggression rather than affection, successfully designed to discomfit him and break his confidence with her onstage. Beautiful young men in the theatre world are, in this book, portrayed through the lens of the mild contempt that Karen Stone felt for all of them: they were, at best, props for her to enhance her performance as an actress, nothing more. The reversal of this in Rome, where she is reduced to lusting after and paying for meals, clothes and drinks for the sort of young men she would never have given a moment's thought to back in America, is all part of her tragedy.

More than sixty years after it was published, the book has an extra resonance, in that it foretold, with great psychological accuracy, the fundamental emotional truth in Williams's life and in the plots of a number of his plays, particularly *Sweet Bird of Youth*. He (who, despite never being a great looker, easily found sex as a young man, and who became far more of a figure in the theatre world than the fictional Karen Stone) was sometimes reduced in his later years to begging the current young man in his life to accompany him to dinner, let alone on one of his endless trips abroad – trips where he seemed, like Mrs Stone, to be desperately avoiding the drift.

The real-life relationship that gave Tennessee the inspiration for *The Roman Spring of Mrs Stone* was not with a young aristocrat but with a seventeen-year-old boy, Salvatore, who was much closer to the description of the nameless stalker than to Paolo. Picking him up outside a patisserie, where the boy had been sitting at a pavement table, in effect offering himself to passers-by, Williams took him back to the Hotel Ambasciatori where he was staying. This took some nerve, as the boy's coat was almost falling apart and his shoes were tied to his feet to keep them from disintegrating.

Giving the staff a generous tip to turn a blind eye, he took the boy to his room but, astonishingly, nothing happened that night. Salvatore – whom Tennessee called Rafaello in his memoirs – was under the control of a tyrannical father and wanted to be sure that, if he started an affair with the American writer, he would be able to leave his father's house for ever. Williams agreed to help him and moved out of the hotel into a serviced apartment whose caretaker provided room service, cheerfully bringing up breakfast which Salvatore devoured while Williams stuck to a liquid meal of black coffee. The boy was bought a new set of clothes and shoes and provided with a cheap hotel room, alternating his nights between there and the apartment. Even after the relationship came to its inevitable end, Williams continued to send him money and take an interest in him – a case of affection transforming what could have been a casually mercenary arrangement into a genuine friendship.

On its publication in 1950, *The Roman Spring of Mrs Stone* scandalized Italian high society. Its members were used to books about the splendour of the Eternal City, or press articles about the latest fashions, and as such they were appalled at the representation of their city as a place of elegant prostitution – and, even worse, the prostitution of young men. Sexual relations on a summer's evening, in private, between tourists and Romans was one thing. For a world-famous playwright to write about them in print was quite another. Ironically, to mark his seventieth birthday (31 years after the book was published), Williams was presented with an award for literary accomplishment by Bulgari, the Italian jewellers. He was amused at the volte-face and pleased that the award – jewellery – was actually worth something in terms of 'scrap' value.

Although *The Roman Spring of Mrs Stone* was based on his experience with Salvatore, it also reflected other trips to the city, including those with Frank Merlo who by now had become his life partner. They had first met in Provincetown, Massachusetts, in 1947. On that occasion, they had picked each other up for casual sex on the sand dunes. They were to meet again, purely by chance, in New York, where Frank confided that he had not wanted to follow up their first encounter as he did not want to seem to be a gold-digger. As an ex-sailor without much money, the financial and social gap between him and a rising (indeed, risen) star playwright seemed too large: it would be, financially, an unequal relationship. Tennessee brushed this objection aside and the two became lovers and then partners for the next fourteen or so years, finally splitting up in 1961, the year of *The Night of the Iguana*. That the split and the opening of his last major critical and commercial success came at about the same time was no coincidence. The period between their break-up and Frank's death, from lung cancer, in 1963, saw a rapid increase in the writer's intake of drink and drugs. Frank's death sent Tennessee into a state of chronic depression, worsened and lengthened by his drug and alcohol abuse.

All this, however, was a long way off when the two met. Though Williams continued to have casual sex with other men, Frank brought some stability and a constant and reassuring affection into his life. Williams had clearly been able to produce great work before the two met, but their relationship proved to be an essential background to the writer's continued development, industry and output through the golden period of his career – a period that, as mentioned above, coincided with their relationship. Frank struck friends of the couple as a decent and honourable man, as well as being physically attractive and a very good organizer. A private secretary as well as a lover, he organized his partner's life and gave him such domestic happiness as he ever enjoyed. He took understandable pride in doing so. In a meeting with a Hollywood executive, Merlo was asked what he did. His reply, which left the executive speechless, was straightforward: 'I sleep with Mr Williams.'

Merlo's family was originally from Sicily. This added spice to Tennessee's love for Italy and its culture and encouraged him to continue his trips there as often as possible. The most direct link between personal and professional life manifested itself in 1951, when his next major play, *The Rose Tattoo*, opened in New York after a run in Chicago. He later described the work as 'my love play to the world. It was permeated with the happy young love for Frankie.' As

Tennessee Williams and his long-term Italian-American lover, Frank Merlo –
nicknamed 'Little Horse'.

befitted something inspired by the early stages of a fulfilling love affair, it was, for once, cheerful and optimistic.

The Rose Tattoo is set in a fictional coastal town in Louisiana, in an area of the United States noted for its large Italian immigrant population. Though American, this play has a strong Italian feel to it. Suffused with images of roses, its principal character is Serafina Delle Rose, a fiery thirty-something Italian immigrant. She loses her husband, Rosario, a sexually charged truck driver, when he is shot (he has a criminal sideline to his work) by rival gangsters. The news causes her to miscarry and seems to herald the end of her sex life and the loneliness of widowhood. All that seemed vital and alive – her passionate relationship with her husband, the new life growing within her – has been lost.

So far, so Tennessee Williams, in the sense of a drama about tragedy and loss. However, *The Rose Tattoo* shows, unequivocally, the power of the human spirit to rise above adversity. Serafina finds a new lover, whose dark hair and rugged good looks are remarkably like those of her late husband, while her daughter Rosa, whom Serafina at first discourages from having sex with her boyfriend, a sailor named Jack, goes on to consummate their relationship before marriage yet still wins Serafina's blessing. This blessing comes after her daughter has discovered that her mother has spent the night with her handsome lover, whose courtship of her – a typical Williams combination of sex and humour – has revitalized the woman.

The Rose Tattoo is a portrayal of a vibrant Italian community and a celebration of heat, sun and sexual passion. Despite some dark moments, it is a happy, life-affirming piece that celebrates the best in Mediterranean culture. As such it is a generalized expression of the very specific pleasure Tennessee found in his relationship with Frank. His nickname for his lover was Little Horse. This was partly a reference to Frank's compact size – muscular but small – but has also been variously attributed to his large teeth and to the impressive size of his private parts. Tennessee wrote an affectionate though

rather wistful poem about him, called 'Little Horse', whose opening
lines are:

> *Mignon* he was or *mignonette*
> *Avec les yeux plus grands que lui.*
> My name for him was Little Horse.
> I fear he had no name for me.

The French words that open the poem are translatable as 'Cute
he was or even pretty / With eyes bigger than the rest of him.'

Poetry came naturally to Williams and was, as discussed
earlier, a long-standing interest of his. His first collection of
poems, published in 1956, was called *In The Winter of Cities.*
Among them was 'Covenant', about the implicit agreement
between two lovers:

> If you are happy, I will give you an apple,
> if you are anxious, I will twist your arm,
> and if you permit me, I will be glad to hold you,
> close to my heart forever and do you no harm.

In 1953, two years after *The Rose Tattoo,* his next play, *Camino
Real,* opened in New York in March. It closed in May, after some
sixty performances. The problem was that it was wildly avant-garde,
a succession of scenes against the surreal setting of a Mexican town
peopled by characters from history and literature – and occasionally,
with Lord Byron for example, both.

Camino Real had a dreamlike quality that belonged more to
the drug culture and experimental theatre world of the late 1960s
than to the Broadway of the early 1950s. As such, it surprised and
dismayed critics and public alike. A touch of the poetic was fine with
them, provided it was staged within a recognizable structure with a
clear plot line. *Camino Real* was the extreme opposite of this, set in

an unreal environment where disparate characters struggled to escape into a more real world beyond its boundaries.

In this play, Williams blended fantasy with a critique of American capitalism and a prevailing culture more interested in making money than in freeing the spirit – a society where dissent is stamped out. Set against the background of McCarthyism, the period when frenzied efforts were made to find communists in all walks of life and to freeze them out of any positions of influence, especially cultural influence and specifically the film industry, *Camino Real* seemed to some of the public to be guilty of the very 'anti-American' ideas that Senator Joseph McCarthy was so determined to root out.

Another bête noire of the senator was homosexuality – as it was of the British establishment. The year 1953, when *Camino Real* appeared, was when the British home secretary, David Maxwell Fyfe, pursed a vigorous campaign against homosexuals, including the court case against Lord Montagu of Beaulieu, Peter Wildeblood and Michael Pitt-Rivers, who were prosecuted and sent to prison for participating in consensual gay sex. Wildeblood's memoir of the trial and imprisonment, *Against the Law* (1955), was hugely influential in Britain and played a major part in the subsequent Wolfenden Report. This was a public inquiry which, in 1957, recommended the decriminalization of homosexuality in England. The Report's recommendations were not implemented until ten years later, but there was some consolation for those at the receiving end of intolerance and persecution in 1953, to know that their example had led to the exact opposite of what their prosecutors had wanted.

Throughout this period (and indeed until 1968) the English stage was, astonishingly, still subject to official censorship by the Lord Chamberlain, a member of the royal household. Homosexuality was one of the taboo subjects for theatre performance, so any reference to it had to be coded or played down. In light of this censorship, plays that addressed forbidden subjects had, when staged in London, to be performed in theatre clubs, which legally required the audience to be members. This was how, for example, Robert Anderson's *Tea and Sympathy*, which dealt with homosexuality, was first shown in England.

Fortunately, there was no such restriction on Broadway, so Williams was free – subject to the commercial constraints of what audiences would accept – to examine, in his plays, something that was central to his own life and sense of self. Despite this, the cultural environment in which he worked meant that the topic had to be handled with some care, and in both *A Streetcar Named Desire* and his next play, *Cat on a Hot Tin Roof*, the gay characters ended up dead or crippled. This meant that the more puritan theatregoers could have the frisson of hearing about gay people while learning that they had come to satisfactorily unpleasant ends.

Cat on a Hot Tin Roof got its title from a phrase that Cornelius Williams often used, disparagingly rather than affectionately, of his wife Edwina, when she became agitated about his drinking, womanizing or simply late arrival home from work. The play opened at the Morosco Theatre in New York in March 1955 and proved to be one of Williams's most successful plays – and the one he was the most proud of. This did not stop him continuing to work on it later, as with all his plays and stories, while the ending was slightly amended (to more than slight effect), not least because of the influence of Elia Kazan, who directed it. That influence is worth looking at in a little more detail before going on to discuss *Cat on a Hot Tin Roof* itself.

Elia Kazan, who was two years older than Tennessee, was of Greek heritage, though born in Turkey, and arrived with his family as an immigrant to America in 1913. This outsider status and his lack of classic good looks made him resentful of many upper-class, attractive white actors, a resentment that briefly took the form of Communism. His turning against erstwhile colleagues when, as an ex-Communist, he testified against the Party in front of the Communist-hunting House Committee on Un-American Activities in the 1950s, was to seriously damage his standing among the film and theatre establishment for decades.

Though he was to become one of America's most noted film directors, with work that included *A Streetcar Named Desire, On the Waterfront* (both with Marlon Brando) and *East of Eden* (with James Dean), he began his extraordinary career in the theatre, first as an actor, then as a director. A member, as was his wife, of the socially aware Group Theatre – the organization that gave a crucial early grant to Tennessee – Kazan was also a founder of the Actors Studio. This studio encouraged the acting technique known as method acting – where performance came from inside the actor, with a total identification with the role, rather than the more conventional application of acting techniques and skill to a part from the outside, as it were – and was to revolutionize theatre on both sides of the Atlantic (not that there did not exist some resistance to this, or fun poked at it by those from an earlier tradition). When Noël Coward, while directing a play, was asked by a young actor who was unsure quite how to play a part, 'What's my motivation at this point, Mr Coward?', Coward replied, scathingly, 'Your pay cheque on Friday.'

Those who have no experience of working in the theatre often assume that a play arrives on a producer's desk, that the producer chooses a director, and that they both pick a cast. The actors and director then mount the production onstage, with not a word changed – the only discussion around the words being how best to say them and how and where to move when doing so. The reality is very different. Over the course of rehearsals, which usually last for approximately four weeks, directors and indeed actors will often ask writers for changes or adaptations in response to certain scenes not working as well as they might, or to make characterization or plot more understandable or effective. That these changes to the script – and sometimes to the plot line – are a normal part of this process is reflected in the fact that a standard theatre contract states that any changes to the script in rehearsal (an actor may improve on a line, for example, with a suggestion of his own) become, automatically, the copyright of the author.

The fact that Elia Kazan worked on four of Tennessee's plays – *A Streetcar Named Desire*, *Camino Real*, *Cat on a Hot Tin Roof* and *Sweet Bird of Youth* – shows that they got on well. Kazan's input was important in all four cases, and he was never backward in suggesting changes to the playwright. The problem was that Williams increasingly resented the input because he felt that rather than making tweaks to the play, Kazan had his own ideas as to how they should have been written in the first place: in other words, Kazan wanted to be involved in the development of plot as much as the performance of it. *Cat on a Hot Tin Roof* was a case in point. As originally written, Brick refuses to go along with Maggie's machinations to provide an heir. Her desire to do so is yet another part of the mendacity – in this instance, meaning hypocrisy as well as untruth – that Brick rails against in the play. Kazan wanted a more emotionally satisfying and therefore commercial end to the play, with the suggestion that Brick has relented and the two of them will indeed sleep together and have a child. The author's dislike of being bullied, as he saw it, by his director, led him to have both endings published when the script appeared in book form, and he also spoke in public about his sense of betrayal in being forced to compromise his artistic principles on this and other plays. Normally, his art reflected his life: here, as he sounded like Brick complaining about a world of mendacity, life imitated art.

The two men's collaboration was to end after *Sweet Bird of Youth*, partly because Williams had burned his bridges by publicly airing his dissatisfaction with Kazan's input into his work, but also because Kazan himself was aware that there was some truth in the writer's complaints: that he *did* want more direct influence on scripts than a world-famous writer might be happy with – and that he would prefer to concentrate on film, where the director is much more in charge of

Theatre and film director Elia Kazan.

the finished product than he or she is with a play. Though their paths would diverge professionally, they remained good friends.

Cat on a Hot Tin Roof is set on a Southern plantation, in Mississippi, in the grand colonial-style house of Big Daddy Pollitt, a self-made multimillionaire, who is dying of cancer – although he has been told the opposite, in a misguided attempt to avoid spoiling his birthday celebrations. Big Daddy's legacy is being fought over by two women:

Mae Pollitt and Maggie – also known as Maggie the Cat. Mae is the wife of Gooper (the less attractive of Big Daddy's sons), has already produced several children and is determined that the estate be left to her husband, having proved they can carry on the family line. She is pitted against the glamorous figure of Maggie, the wife of Brick, Big Daddy's other son. Brick is a strikingly attractive former athletics champion who has taken to the bottle. He refuses to sleep with his wife, as he blames her for the death of Skipper, his best friend, who committed suicide some time before the action begins. Played out against the background of a thunderstorm that mirrors the electric tension and occasional explosive exchanges within the family, *Cat on a Hot Tin Roof* is a superb drama, with, at its heart, Brick's (and the author's) railing against 'mendacity' – the lies that most people tell themselves and others in order to get through life, but which render that life intolerable for anyone with a conscience or any sensitivity of spirit.

Mendacity may be the issue that Brick rails against, but another, more personal one is the question of his sexuality. Skipper, we learn, was gay. When he had tried to prove the contrary – in reaction to Maggie's taunts about the nature of his affection for Brick – by having sex with her, he unsurprisingly failed. That, and Brick's rejection of him when he finally declared a love that must have been obvious to both of them and was also reciprocated (though it would never have been consummated) by Brick, had led Skipper to kill himself.

With his broken leg and reliance on crutches as a metaphor for a broken heart and self-crippled masculinity, Brick might be a pathetic sight, but his physical charms and the strength of Maggie's passion for him, despite his frequent rejection of her, means that he continues to be a broodingly attractive figure. He is also, of course, the potential heir to a vast fortune, if Big Daddy can be persuaded to see his once-favourite son as anything but a drunken loser. This begs the question of whether Maggie's desire, however genuine, is at least partly fuelled by the prospect of wealth and status, as well as a

Poster for the film version of *Cat on a Hot Tin Roof* (1958), showing Elizabeth Taylor in her prime. There is some debate as to whether the play 'belongs' to her character, Maggie the Cat, or her husband Brick (played on-screen by Paul Newman), but the poster leaves no doubt as to who the producers thought the public wanted to see.

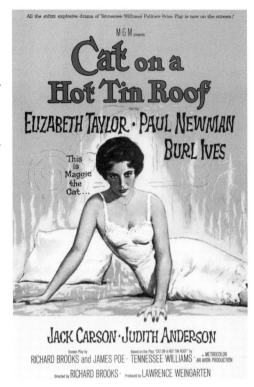

renewed sex life with a handsome man. For Maggie has an astute awareness of the need for money in life, especially when one loses the only other worthwhile currency – youth. As she tells Brick, 'You can be young without money but you can't be old without it.'

At the end of the play, Maggie announces (in a stunningly effective example of mendacity) that she is carrying Brick's child, and that he – having re-bonded with his father in the course of the evening – and she are therefore worthy to be heirs to the family estate. What she certainly has proved is her own suitability for such a role, though in the Deep South in the 1950s any woman, however strong and suitable, can only exercise power through her husband.

The open reference to homosexuality shocked many people, but by now audiences knew that a Tennessee Williams play involved frank – and often tempestuous – examinations of the human heart. This frankness and ability to push boundaries was acceptable onstage but far less so on-screen.

The following year, 1956, saw the release of a film called *Baby Doll*, an amalgamation of two one-act plays, *27 Wagons Full of Cotton* and *The Long Stay Cut Short, or The Unsatisfactory Supper*. The film, starring Carroll Baker and Eli Wallach as a farmer with a much younger, very sexy wife (there was a lot of suggestive thumb-sucking going on) attempted to put sexuality as blatantly into the cinema as the playwright was now used to doing onstage. The resulting outcry, led by the Roman Catholic Church in America, did wonders for the box office. Surprisingly, the film had a supporter in the form of Cornelius Coffin. His sister, Tennessee's aunt Ella, took her nephew to one side at Cornelius's funeral the following year and showed him

Tennessee Williams in front of a camera at the premiere of *Baby Doll* (1956).

a photo of Cornelius outside a cinema where *Baby Doll* was playing. Writing in his essay 'The Man in the Overstuffed Chair' in the 1960s, the playwright proudly recalled that on the back of the photo Cornelius had written 'I think it's a very fine picture and I'm proud of my son.'

Baby Doll is an example of how Tennessee adapted work from one format (short stories, one-act plays) into another: full-length plays or films. In doing so, he would sometimes quite radically adapt plots, while retaining their essential cores. This was the case, for example, with *Orpheus Descending* (a reworking of *Battle of Angels*), which made even clearer the parallels with the classical myth of Orpheus descending to Hades to reclaim his dead wife and bring her back to sunlight and life – almost making it, but losing her just before she reached the safety of the world above ground. The play has Christian as well as classical symbolism and in this, as with the heightened sense of drama and the shockingly violent ending, the play has the feel of an opera, not least because the central character, Val (the Orpheus figure), is a musician.

Val is a handsome drifter who arrives in a small town where Lady Torrance is a frustrated thirty-something woman married to an older, unattractive man (echoes of *Baby Doll*) called Jabe. Lady runs a store. She is an Italian immigrant (another nod to the playwright's relationship with Frank Merlo), whose father was burnt to death, some years ago, when his lakeside restaurant and bar were set on fire by a thuggish mob of rednecks who objected to him serving African Americans as well as whites. She is unaware, when the play opens, that her husband, Jabe Torrance, was one of the main instigators of this, though she discovers it in the course of the drama.

The play makes clear that violence is far from past in the South. The racism that led to the fire-bombing of Lady's father's business is still on display, in the language and actions displayed by the locals. The frequent use of the word 'nigger' would have been less shocking in 1957 than it is today, but the context in which it occurs and the vehemence with which it is used makes it clear that these are not just casual racists. That the lynch mob mentality still rules is demonstrated in another context. Carol Cutrere comes from the local wealthy family, but she has been given an informal yet inflexibly administered ban on visiting the area after she took an interest in civil rights. Over thirty years old (which in his plays is a very dangerous birthday to have passed, especially for a woman), she has a ruined beauty which makes her mental – or at least moral – instability all the more poignant. In another sign of her distance from mainstream society she is far more comfortable than the other local women in talking to African Americans. This unusual (among the locals) ease with people of other races suggests that, despite her implied waywardness, she is a fundamentally decent person. Her family pay her to stay away from town, but public opinion is the enforcer of the social mores. Williams's use of sound effects – specifically, the howls of dogs let loose to find a runaway convict from a chain gang, and the savage snarling when they find him and tear him apart – helps further in painting a background of savage behaviour directed against anyone who transgresses social codes.

Val Xavier arrives at Lady's store, brought by Vee Talbot, a middle-aged artist who is somewhat improbably married to the thuggish local sheriff. Vee has (and then paints) religious visions. Val, whose thirtieth birthday it is, is a stock Tennessee Williams male leading man, in that he was once a gorgeous youth, is now older but still handsome and causes as much instant excitement in the store as a new cockerel in a hen house.

Lady, who decides to employ him and eventually offers to let him sleep behind a curtain in an alcove at the back of the store, is initially resistant to his charms: 'I'm not interested in your perfect functions, in fact you don't interest me no more than the air that you stand in. If that's understood, we'll have a good working relation, but otherwise trouble!' Her statement is prophetic, though it is she who initiates what becomes a sexual relationship, with

The highly regarded Bunkamura theatre, Tokyo, production of *Orpheus Descending*.

disastrous consequences. Val's sex appeal has been his strength, but it is now his greatest vulnerability, because in a place like this, women throw themselves at or gossip about him, while their husbands are instantly antagonistic, whatever he does.

Things come to a head when he is unjustly accused by two men: the sheriff and Jabe. The sheriff has already misinterpreted Val's holding of his wife's hand and comes into the store when Val is consoling Vee, who has been upset by a particularly violent and intense vision. Claiming that Christ touched her heart, she places Val's hand on her chest to show him exactly how Christ laid his hand on her. Seeing this, the sheriff wrongly assumes that Val is touching her sexually. In the play's denouement, Val learns that he has made Lady pregnant. Following this, a furious, hate-filled Jabe shoots Lady and then, out of the malice that has been the main motivating force of his whole life, shouts out that he caught Val trying to rob the store, and that Val, cornered, has shot Lady. Eagerly responding to this, the sheriff and his friends, who have already roughed Val up once before and ordered him out of town, rush into the store, chase Val outside and, in a peculiarly unpleasant touch – as much Tarantino as Tennessee – kill him (offstage, mercifully) with a blowtorch.

This death by fire is a deliberate echo of the fate that befell Lady's father. It suggests that any outsider, whether an Italian immigrant or a sexually challenging young man, has to be 'cleansed' by flames. That the action is set over the Easter weekend gives more than a suggestion of Christian imagery, with Val as the blameless Christ figure. Val certainly brings a message of love with him – and the need to reach out to others. He says to Lady, 'We're all of us sentenced to solitary confinement inside our own skins, for life!' What he seems to offer is a chance for Lady to reconnect with the world, and thus with life. The importance of grasping life is made clear by Carol Cutrere, when she is trying to persuade him to have sex with her:

> Take me out to Cypress Hill in my car. And we'll hear the dead people talk. They do talk there. They chatter together like birds on Cypress Hill, but all they say is one word and that one word is 'live', they say 'Live, live, live, live, live!' It's all they've learned, it's the only advice they can give . . .

Val brings new life to Lady in the form of the child growing within her, but the promise of a fresh start is gunned down. This last-minute ending of the promise of a new beginning is Williams's version of the myth's tragic conclusion. In the original, Orpheus is granted permission by Hades, god of the Underworld, to take Orpheus' wife, Eurydice, back up to the world and to a second chance of life. The sole condition is that he not look back. At the very last moment, just before he emerges into the sunlight, Orpheus, overwhelmed by love, cannot resist looking over his shoulder to check that Eurydice really is with him. The moment he does so, she, who has been following behind him, is lost forever.

Val, like Orpheus, is portrayed as a musician. His guitar is his most prized possession, and he sings gently and movingly in the course of the play. The small town he finds himself in is certainly hellish, and he brings to it the promise of escape. In the myth the fault is that of Orpheus, for looking back and therefore losing the future. In Williams's play, the role is reversed in that it is Lady who is destroyed by looking back, in the sense of being unable to forget the past and focus entirely on the future. Val wants to leave, but she is determined to avenge her father's death by recreating something of his lakeside pleasure garden inside her own shop. As a result, she stays there far too long, meets her doom at the hand of her vile husband and unwittingly brings to her lover the same sort of death as her father's all those years ago.

Critics and audiences disliked the violence of *Orpheus Descending* when it opened in New York in March 1957, and were affronted at the Christian theme, especially in view of the Easter setting. Williams was badly shaken by the reaction to the play. It is thought to have been a determining factor in his decision to undergo psychoanalysis with a leading practitioner, Dr Lawrence S. Kubie. This was a process he loathed and gratefully abandoned, preferring to battle his demons through his typewriter. As he said in an interview several years earlier with an English newspaper (*The Observer*) when *A Streetcar Named Desire* opened in London, 'I guess my work has always been a kind of psychotherapy for me.'

In 'The Man in the Overstuffed Chair', a portrait of his father (written around 1960, though not published until 1980) in which he showed remarkable if belated sympathy for Cornelius, Tennessee made the surprisingly frank admission that

For love I make characters in plays. To the world I give suspicion and resentment, mostly . . . I have little to give but indifference to people. I try to excuse myself with the pretence that my work justifies this lack of caring much for almost anything else. Sometimes I crack through the emotional block. I touch, I embrace, I hold tight to a necessary companion. But the breakthrough is not long lasting. Morning returns, and only work matters again.

Clinging to this, he was, though upset at the reaction to the play, resolutely defiant in his belief that his writing was ahead of its time rather than substandard.

Orpheus Descending once again showed how strongly he was influenced by his lifelong fascination with classical culture. The play owes its origins to other ancient Greek myths and theatre in addition to the story of Orpheus and Eurydice. There are also shades of Euripides' *The Bacchae* and the tearing to pieces of those who offend the god Dionysus. In *Orpheus Descending*, it is the local rednecks who take the place of intoxicated followers of the god, destroying those who offend against the norm. This image, one of the oldest in European literature, was reworked in an even more extreme way in his next major play, *Suddenly Last Summer*, which opened in New York in January 1958. A tribute to his productivity as much as his talent, this was set in the Garden District of New Orleans and was originally part of a double bill called, appropriately, *Garden District*. The other play was another one-acter called *Something Unspoken*, which is nowadays rarely performed – *Suddenly Last Summer* tends to be produced on its own.

Something Unspoken deserves a mention, however, as it was a skilfully drawn chamber piece featuring two women: Cornelia, who is rich, and Grace, her secretary and companion. The pair are also a couple, though given the social mores of the time there is nothing very open, let alone liberated, about their life together. Their relationship is an emotional rather than a sexual one, and the very fact of its – and their – real nature, the presence of a mutual attraction that is on a different level to that of employer and employee, or of friendship, is the unspoken thing of the play's title. Though several subsidiary clues are present – a record that is a favourite of theirs is by a singer known to be a lesbian, for instance – the overall tone of the play is quiet, gentle: a complete contrast to the Grand Guignol horrors that were to follow in the second half of the double bill. The connection between the two parts of the evening, despite the wholly different tones, was that it is not always necessary to bring the truth about sexual feelings into the open, summed up in a line from the first of the two plays: 'You say there's something unspoken. Maybe there is. I don't know. But I do know some things are better left unspoken.'

In *Suddenly Last Summer*, Mrs Venables, a wealthy society matron, has lost her son, a gay poet called Sebastian, on a visit he made to Europe with his cousin, Catharine. The girl claims he was a promiscuous gay who met a shocking end brought on by his sexual predations on young men. In order to silence her niece, Mrs Venables wants a young doctor to carry out a lobotomy on her. This threat is the most direct reference Williams makes in his work to the procedure carried out on his sister. In the play, as in real life, the threat comes from an overbearing mother figure wanting any challenge from a young woman to the respectability and reputation of the family to be literally cut off at the source. In real life, Williams was unable to prevent his mother from having Rose's brain sliced apart. In the theatre, he was able to parade the horror of such a procedure, while at the same time ensuring that, unlike in life, the young woman is saved from this horrible fate.

Sebastian's even more ghastly end, which Mrs Venables wants to keep secret, had come when he was set upon by a crowd of the adolescents he had been in the habit of having paid sex with on the sand dunes. Not only did they gang together to kill him by tearing him apart, they also ate the flesh that had abused them. The imagery is all the more shocking for being described rather than shown – another case of classical influence, as violence was always offstage in ancient Greek drama. In the film version, a more literal, on-screen representation was given, much to Tennessee's fury.

Extreme violence was also in store for the male protagonist in Williams's next play, *Sweet Bird of Youth*, starring Geraldine Page

Katherine Hepburn as the terrifying Mrs Venables in the film version of *Suddenly Last Summer* (1959).

and Paul Newman, both Tennessee Williams veterans. It opened
at the Martin Beck Theatre in New York in 1959, three years after
an initial try-out in Florida. *Sweet Bird of Youth* is a powerful exam-
ination of the impact of failed ambitions, lost love and the cruelty,
corruption and bigotry that were the dark side of the American
South. The play is typically tragic and with over-the-top violence
that showed, once again, the influence of Greek myths on Williams's
work: the main character is castrated at the end of the play. Yet it
also offers a sense of redemption and reward, as the lead female
character, an ageing Hollywood star called Alexandra Del Lago (also
known, when travelling incognito, as the Princess Kosmonopolis),
seemingly down on her luck, finds that her latest film, which she
thought was a humiliating failure, has turned out to be a success.
Therefore she can, for now at least, resume her career.

Superficially, the play's central character is Chance Wayne,
a late twenty-something small-town boy. As a teenager, Chance

Geraldine Page and Paul Newman as a film star and the gigolo she picks up in *Sweet
Bird of Youth* (1962).

was stunningly good-looking and seemed, thanks to his youth and beauty, to have a golden future ahead of him. The reality was very different, and he has come back to his home town in the hope of recapturing past glories and making a fresh start with his one-time sweetheart, an equally attractive girl called Heavenly. That this dream is doomed becomes apparent very quickly. After all, he has returned home not as someone who has made it in the wider world, but as a gigolo, brought to town by Alexandra Del Lago who needs companionship and the compensations of sex after running away from the premiere of her latest film.

Heavenly's father is Boss Finley, the local politician and landowner. A brutal and corrupt man, his political campaign forms a backdrop to the action and gives a graphic display of the worst of Southern bigotry and violence. This, more usually directed against African Americans and those who support them, is now focused on Chance. The reason is twofold: as the apparently virginal daughter (dressed demurely in white) of a powerful man, Heavenly is a convenient symbol of white female purity for Boss Finley when on the campaign trail. Having her reputation besmirched by association with a no-hope, would-be actor and part-time gigolo is the last thing he wants. More personally, it turns out that Chance, when he was last in town, had given Heavenly a venereal disease. Diagnosed at a late stage, in part due to her ignorance about such matters, she had to have a hysterectomy. As well as the physical reality, the operation represents an evisceration of everything Heavenly appears to be – both for her father and for Chance. The image she presents of youthful femininity, the promise she therefore offers of romantic love, fertility and a future family, is a sham. Just as Chance's dream of a future as a Hollywood actor is a self-deceiving fantasy.

Heavenly's brother, a thug whose righteous indignation at his sister's fate is largely an excuse for violence, threatens that, unless he leaves town, Chance will be castrated. By the time Alexandra realizes that her premiere was, in fact, a hit, and that her career has a new lease of life, Chance's own hopes have died. Her future transformed, Alexandra no longer has any need of him, and she dismisses his deluded expectation that she will help get him an acting job. She does, however, offer to take him with her, to save him from Finley's henchmen, but Chance, defeated, chooses to stay. The play ends with him directly addressing the audience with the acknowledgement that Time is the great enemy of humanity: 'I don't ask for your pity, but just for your understanding – not even that – no. Just for your recognition of me in you, and the enemy, time, in us all.'

Though the tragedy is Chance's, it is Alexandra Del Lago who is the most interesting, most powerful character – so much so that *Sweet Bird of Youth*'s flaw is her absence in Act II, or, rather, her reduction from worldly wise and amusingly sympathetic character in Acts I and III, to a more-or-less walk-on part as a middle-aged woman desperately looking for her missing gigolo. As a result, Act II, though it tells us more about Chance's back story, is less satisfactory than the acts that precede and follow it. The political drama – Tennessee's presentation of redneck Southern racism and violence in the form of Boss Finley's campaign rally – though topical, lacks the sureness of touch and audience involvement that marks his treatment of more personal, intimately staged situations.

It is in these staged situations that Alexandra shines, sometimes through a cynical humour, sometimes through sheer grit. Though Chance is doomed to lose his, it is she, of the two of them, who has the balls. Like other Williams female characters, she is past her prime in terms of looks and career. She knows this and suffers accordingly, but is, at heart, a fighter. One does not become a Hollywood star by being delicate, and she proves to have, along with a strong sex drive, a more masculine approach to life than Chance.

In a reversal of traditional roles, the man is the beautiful one who cannot get over the loss of youth and looks; the woman is the fighter, the ballsy alcohol-soaked bruiser who won't give up without a fight. The contrast between the way she pulls herself together to have another go at life and Chance's effete acceptance of the savage severing (literally) of his manhood makes for powerful theatre. Though Chance's fate is horrendous, the audience does not feel much more than sadness. There is nothing gut-wrenching about what is about to happen to him because he is too weak really to attract our sympathy. Alexandra, by contrast, lifts the spirits. Because she has survived, the play's ultimate message is an uplifting one, of renewal and moving on.

In a sense, then, Williams undermines the tragedy of the play, but Chance's weakness points up Alexandra's strength of spirit, which we cannot help but admire. By giving her hope and the audience something to look forward to, on her behalf, he makes a public statement of his own credo: that work is what counts most in life and that the show must, while life lasts, go on. This was summed up by his favourite (and inevitably European) phrase: 'En avant!' (Forwards!). As Alexandra did, Tennessee took to booze and pills and paid companionship, but as she did he too could be lifted from hysteria or despair by the slightest hint of success. His self-worth, like hers, was dependent on the way his work was received. He was, in 1959, only a couple of years from the end of his run of hits and ahead of him were twenty years of increasingly bruising failure, relieved only by the occasional semi-success. However, throughout these years he would continue, religiously – and at times almost manically – to work. He never gave up hope that he, like Miss Del Lago, might wake one day in a hotel bedroom, with a handsome hustler at his side, to receive a telephone call that would announce his resurrection as an artist.

Sweet Bird of Youth's depiction of the violent underside of American politics echoed the political commitment of some of his earliest plays. It was a backdrop to the personal tragedies being played out onstage rather than a focal point, but its inclusion was curiously prophetic of the greatly increased political consciousness of America (and Europe) in the decade to come.

4

The 1960s: A Period of Adjustment

A Period of Adjustment, Tennessee's first play of the 1960s, had
a prophetic title. This was to be a decade of enormous change,
not just in America but across the world, with the beginning of the
Vietnam War, mass student unrest, civil rights marches and political
assassinations – including those of President Kennedy, his brother
Senator Robert Kennedy (a presidential candidate when gunned
down) and Martin Luther King, Jr. It was also to be a highly
traumatic decade for Tennessee Williams, during which he would
see a string of plays turned into films but have his new work (after
The Night of the Iguana, of which more later) attacked by critics as
they switched from promoters to persecutors. A strong word, and
one which might seem to reflect the growing paranoia he suffered
during these years, but his treatment by them amounted to more
than just a change of fashion – it was as if they took personal affront
against his new plays and more modern style of writing.

A Period of Adjustment opened at the Helen Hayes Theater in New
York in November 1960. A light comedy of manners rather than a
direct attack on American society – even though it satirizes aspects
of it – it has its share of dark undertones, reminiscent of the work
of the prolific English playwright Sir Alan Ayckbourn. The play
describes the marital troubles of a middle-aged couple, Ralph and
Dorothy, and newly-weds, Isabel and George, who have come to
stay with them. Ralph and Dorothy's house sits on a cave and is
gradually sinking into it, hence the play's alternative title, *High Point*

Cast of *The Night of the Iguana* (1961). Legendary film star Bette Davis was persuaded to appear in the Broadway production as hotel owner Maxine Faulk.

is Built on a Cavern. For the time, it was a sexually explicit play – not for what it showed (it was relatively demure), but for discussions between the characters about impotence, the need for tenderness in sex and the potential problems of the marital bed. The importance of the sexual side of a marriage had also been highlighted by Big Mamma when talking to Maggie in *Cat on a Hot Tin Roof.* Pointing at Brick and Maggie's double bed, she says to her, 'When a marriage goes on the rocks, the rocks are *there*, right *there*!' At the time, women might have been expected to have such discussions in private. They were rarer – onstage and in real life – among heterosexual middle-class men, so in *Period of Adjustment* he was breaking new ground.

His next play, *The Night of the Iguana* of 1961, had a far more exotic location than the American suburbs. It is set in a seaside hotel in Mexico, based on one that he himself stayed in during one of his periodic attempts to escape the United States. *The Night of the Iguana* is about a defrocked priest turned tourist tour leader who finds himself washed up in a coastal resort in a hotel under whose wooden terrace local boys have tied up an iguana. The reptile's fate – trapped and probably doomed by the unthinking and unsympathetic – mirrors that of the man, for Lawrence Shannon is, briefly, tied to a hammock, as much a prisoner as the iguana itself. The seaside hotel is run by Maxine Faulk, a gutsy middle-aged woman who is as much in command of her own little establishment as Rick Blaine was in the film *Casablanca*. The latter character was played by Humphrey Bogart, while Williams's female creation was played onstage – in what seems like an inspired, highly commercial piece of casting – by another legendary movie star: Bette Davis. There have been many female film stars who have happily appeared in Tennessee Williams plays. Unfortunately, Miss Davis wasn't one of them. As monstrous to the other actors as she could manage, she proved a nightmare to work with, and the experience was an unhappy one for the writer, too.

In consideration of his track record with life, Williams should not have been surprised, even if he was disappointed. The play itself struck a chord, however, as the characters were strongly drawn. The second female role, Hannah Jelkes, played gracefully by Margaret Leighton, was one of quiet dignity and strength. Hannah is travelling with her grandfather, Nonno, the world's oldest living poet, who, aged 97, is composing – in his mind rather than on paper – his final poem, his swan song. Audiences were back on familiar Williams territory, even if the setting was more exotic than usual. The Mexican background may have been different but the metaphorical clock still hung over it. Nonno addresses time in one of his poems, which Hannah helps him remember:

> Youth must be wanton, youth must be quick,
> Dance to the candle, while lasteth the wick,

Youth must be foolish and mirthful and blind,
Gaze not before and glance not behind,

Mark not the shadow that darkens the way –
Regret not the glitter of any lost day,

But laugh with no reason except the red wine,
For youth must be youthful and foolish and blind!

The rhymes are rather rum-ti-tum. The subject was dealt with more melodically in one of his other poems, 'We Have Not Long To Love':

We have not long to love.
Light does not stay.
The tender things are those
we fold away.

Coarse fabrics are the ones
for common wear.
In silence I have watched
you comb your hair.

Intimate the silence,
dim and warm.
I could, but did not, reach
to touch your arm.

I could, but do not, break
that which is still.
(Almost the faintest whisper
would be shrill.)

So moments pass as though
they wished to stay.
We have not long to love.
A night. A day . . .

As he liked to do, especially with poetry in the air, Williams
slipped in a reference to Hart Crane. Hannah is an artist. When
Shannon realizes she is sketching him, he asks: 'Are you drawing
me?' and she replies,

Trying to. You're a very difficult subject. When the Mexican
painter Siqueiros did his portrait of the American poet Hart
Crane he had to paint him with closed eyes because he couldn't
paint his eyes open – there was too much suffering in them and
he couldn't paint it.

There is an attractive contrast between the worldly Maxine
and Hannah's calm, supportive personality. Shannon may have
a penchant (and vice versa) for teenage girls – which is how he loses
the tour guide job that brought him to the hotel – but what he longs
for, like the playwright, is company, a connection between two people.
Such a connection is worth compromises, like settling down with
Maxine and running the hotel with her. Hannah, whose whole life
has been a compromise, devoted to looking after her grandfather
and his poetry, loses him at the end when, having completed his last
poem a little earlier, Nonno passes away.

The Night of the Iguana was to be the last of Tennessee Williams's
great successes. This became increasingly apparent as the years went
by, but he refused to accept it, pouring out ideas and forging them
into plays for the rest of his life, hoping to prove his critics wrong.
The pressure he put himself under, exacerbated by a continuing
stream of invective by theatre critics, was made worse over the next
twenty-plus years by the absence of a long-term partner. Having

split up with Frank Merlo in 1961 (Frank deserted Williams for a much younger man, a poet with whom he had a relatively short fling), the two became close again a year or so later, when Frank was diagnosed with lung cancer. Because of his horror of illness in general and hospitals in particular, Tennessee, though he still cared for Frank and had a natural sympathy for his situation, was not well-suited to looking after an invalid. Though he tried his best, taking Frank into his New York apartment when he was on release from chemotherapy treatment in the cancer wards, there was an unhappy tension between the two men.

Writing in his memoirs twelve years later, Williams showed great emotional courage in revealing just how much of a strain this was. He could have painted a picture of loving self-sacrifice, a final coming-together, each relying on the other's affection in the last months of Frank's life. In fact, in what must have been an incredibly difficult passage to write, Williams records that not only did the two men not share a bed (Frank's restlessness at night precluding this), Frank actually locked the bedroom door when he retired for the night to keep his ex-lover out. In the memoirs, Williams asks with bewilderment whether Frank really thought he would have tried to take sexual advantage of him at a time like that. In reality, the locked door was more about the unbridgeable emotional barrier that the playwright's past behaviour had created and Merlo's need to demonstrate, for his own benefit, that he still had some control of his life despite being so close to losing it. A more chilling example of a lack of love and trust, despite accepting physical shelter, would be hard to imagine. Despite, or perhaps because of this, when Merlo finally died, Williams went into a depression that lasted for the rest of the 1960s, leading him deeper into his drug and alcohol habit – hence his nickname for the 1960s, 'the stoned age'. Gore Vidal was to quip that he had not missed anything much.

Even if you are with a new partner, or working your way through a succession of casual encounters or brief affairs, if an ex-partner you are fond of is still around, he is at least a potential source of comfort. He is a reminder of happier times and, subconsciously at least, potentially reclaimable times. Once he has died, however, all such hope and companionship is lost. That, combined with a well-deserved sense of guilt about his handling of their relationship, is why Merlo's death hit Williams so hard. There is also the factor of the playwright's addictive personality. His reaction to the death was one of genuine and at times almost overwhelming grief, but it was as much an excuse for as a cause of the descent into deeper and more prolonged addiction. His ex-lover's passing became an explanation for misery that had actually occurred, at times, during their relationship. His notebooks in the early part of their affair, and indeed all through it, make clear the need he had for sedatives and for drink, even when, according to the generally accepted narrative of his life, he should have been blissfully happy and free from artificial stimulants or chemical escape routes from sadness.

If the vast consumption of these products was needlessly self-destructive and – given his charm, talent and gift for friendship – desperately sad, then what was equally remarkable and admirable was the way, throughout the 'lost' years that followed Merlo's death, in which he resolutely continued to write, every morning, every day. He was financially able to do so not just because of the many productions of his plays, but because of the millions of dollars that came in from their film versions, which were made through the 1950s and '60s. Not unlike the films of Elvis Presley, to which they otherwise bore no comparison, Williams's movies became less well-received as the 1960s wore on, but their cumulative effect was to make him and his style of drama far better known to international audiences than his plays could ever have done on their own.

The year of Frank Merlo's death, 1963, saw the Broadway launch of the play *The Milk Train Doesn't Stop Here Anymore.* Set in Italy, where Williams continued to be a frequent visitor, it had an Italian premiere the year before, at the Festival of Two Worlds in Spoleto.

The play is set in the lavish clifftop villa of the wealthy American widow Flora Goforth on the Italian coast near Capri. Dying of cancer, Mrs Goforth is dictating her memoirs to Blackie, her young female secretary, whom she bullies. Chris Flanders, an attractive young drifter and a published poet who has adopted a nomadic, hippyish lifestyle, arrives at the estate, survives an attack by the guard dogs and is allowed to stay. Chris finds an ally in Blackie, but has a more ambivalent relationship with Mrs Goforth. Despite her age and ill health, she wants him to sleep with her. He refuses. She learns of his reputation as a 'companion' to elderly ladies and his nickname, The Angel of Death. Though he is a real person, he is also, in essence, that mythological figure, and Mrs Goforth dies while Chris sits with her, holding her hand.

The Milk Train Doesn't Stop Here Anymore is considered a minor work but is an enjoyable one for all that, and worth looking at in some detail. It fits snugly into the Williams oeuvre with a leading lady who is a once-beautiful, wealthy widow. It has some witty repartee between duelling divas in the form of Mrs Goforth and her rich neighbour, a woman known as The Witch of Capri. The redneck element also crops up here, in the shape of Mrs Goforth's Head of Security, Rudy, a thuggish man who is secretly stealing from his employer. The dogs that he unleashes on Chris when he first arrives at the estate are distant cousins of those used to attack escaping convicts in *Orpheus Descending*.

When Blackie and Mrs Goforth discuss Chris, Mrs Goforth, talking about him as a type as much as a person, expresses some of the world-weariness with young companions that the playwright felt in the late 1960s and on through the next fifteen years of his life. Replying to her secretary's assertion that 'You must have met him before', Mrs Goforth replies, 'Oh, somewhere, some time, when I was still meeting people, before they all seemed like the same person over and over and I got tired of – the person.' Though she, like women Chris has visited before, is close to death, Mrs Goforth

The Lyric Hammersmith (London) production of *The Milk Train Doesn't Stop Here Anymore*, with Rupert Everett in the role of Mrs Goforth.

retains a life force that will not be denied. When Chris, bemused at her belated attempt to seduce him, compares her body to that of a Scandinavian statue, like those found on their fountains, she immediately replies: 'Yeah, well, baby, a fountain is a stone figure, and my body isn't a stone figure, although its been sculpted by several world-famous sculptors, it's still a flesh and blood figure.' Chris, trying to find a tactful way to explain his resistance to her ancient charms, tries to distance himself from carnality through classical allusions – references that show Williams's knowledge and love of the ancient world of the Mediterranean: 'I admire you

Tennessee with two close friends: Maria Britneva and Gore Vidal.

. . . I think if that old Greek explorer, Pytheas, hadn't beat you to it
by centuries, you would've sailed up through the Gates of Hercules
to map out the Western world.'

Disappointed by Chris's refusal to have sex, Mrs Goforth
accuses him of hoping to wheedle money out of her and snaps:
'You miscalculated with this one. This milk train doesn't stop here
any more.' She then refers to the American tourists who flock to
that part of the world and suggests he try his luck with them. Her
advice, sour though it is, paints a word picture of the south Italian
coast, the sunshine and the sea that have attracted tourists since
Roman times: 'Go back to Naples. Walk along Santa Lucia, the bay
front . . . You'll probably run into some Americans at a sidewalk
table right along there, a party that's in for some shopping from
the islands.'

Just as Williams enjoyed the Italian landscape and people, so did his friend Gore Vidal. Their joint exploration of southern Italy in 1948 has already been touched upon. Vidal, whose work was more austerely intellectual, and primarily novel-based, but whose repartee was every bit as entertaining, eventually settled in Ravello, a little further along the coast from Capri. Vidal's nickname for Tennessee was 'Bird', as he had been struck by how often birds, or bird-like attributes, appeared in his friend's work. There was also a hint of a migratory creature, acknowledging the playwright's constant movement and love of the sun. Vidal and his long-term partner, Howard Austen, were themselves seasonal visitors, regularly spending much of the year in Ravello at their clifftop villa; its dizzy height, with a magnificent view over the Mediterranean, earned it the name La Rondinaia – 'the swallow's nest'.

Another friend was Truman Capote, the novelist, socialite and bon viveur. Capote resembled a Tennessee Williams character in that he too started out life young and cute: a dust jacket photo of him on the back of his novel, *Other Voices, Other Rooms* (1948), looking provocatively sexual caused a storm of protest in more conservative quarters. The gilded youth with precocious talent (he started writing aged eleven) produced two classics, *Breakfast at Tiffany's* (1958) and *In Cold Blood* (1965), but turned, tragically, into a dumpy, bitter man whose amusingly vicious pen portraits of the society ladies who had been his patrons caused them to drop him, casting him adrift from the social life he had so relished. Eventually, succumbing to drug and alcohol abuse, he lost his mind before dying of cancer in 1984, a year after Tennessee. The two had once been good friends, travelling together on the *Queen Mary* back from Italy to America, dodging the attentions of an elderly bishop who, like so many men at the time, had taken a shine to the seductively pretty Capote. Their friendship later soured, and Tennessee mischievously made a direct reference to him in *The Milk Train Doesn't Stop Here Anymore*. Mrs Goforth explains her distrust of strangers by describing a hoax that had been played on her and her wealthy neighbours:

> I've been plagued by impostors lately, the last few summers, the continent has been overrun by impostors of celebrities, writers, actors and so forth. I mean they arrive and say, I am Truman Capote. Well, they look a bit like him so you are taken in by the announcement, I am Truman Capote and you receive him cordially only to find out later that it isn't.

Capote returned the favour in extracts, published in *Esquire* magazine in the mid-1970s, from his unpublished novel *Answered Prayers*. In these he writes about Mr Wallace, a self-pitying, portly, late middle-aged man of slovenly personal habits, who lives in hotel rooms, is usually drunk, has very few friends and spends much of his time and money on rent boys. Ronald Hayman's biography of Tennessee Williams took its title, *Everyone Else is an Audience*, from a line in Capote's character assassination of his one-time friend.

In *The Milk Train Doesn't Stop Here Anymore*, though Chris tells Mrs Goforth they have met before, and though he is evidently not pretending to be famous, she is initially not just wary of him but downright cruel, ignoring his hunger and denying him food. Chris copes with this, just as he ignores her suggestion to turn his attention to other wealthy people in the area. Instead of leaving, he stays with her as she goes to sleep for the final time, saying to him: 'Be here, when I wake up.' For all his poetry, he seems to be the hustler she has accused him of being when he removes the rings from her dying hands, but actually he does so because they cut her fingers as he holds them tightly. He tells Blackie, after Mrs Goforth's death, that he has left the rings with their owner: 'Under her pillow like a pharaoh's breakfast waiting for the pharaoh to wake up hungry.' He then takes the wine that Blackie offers him, his latest mission now accomplished.

Mrs Goforth was played on Broadway by Hermione Baddeley. The part had been written, however, with Tallulah Bankhead in mind. Bankhead, a major star in the 1920s, was by this stage a raddled wreck of her previous self, with a reputation for indulgence in sex, drugs and foul language. Though these traits can be excused – and even have some charm – in the young, they are deeply unattractive in the elderly. Though she had been an element in the inspiration for Blanche DuBois, Lady Torrance in *Orpheus Descending* and Alexandra Del Lago in *Sweet Bird of Youth*, it was no great surprise that Bankhead had not been the first choice to star in any of the roles. She had, however, played Blanche in a revival of *A Streetcar Named Desire* that opened in Florida and transferred to Broadway in 1956, where she had received good reviews, despite Tennessee's deep reservations about her perform- ance. Buoyed by her previous experience and confident of the support of her still considerable (and largely gay) fan base, Tallulah Bankhead was determined to have another crack at a Tennessee Williams heroine. A leading theatre producer, David Merrick, asked the rising English director Tony Richardson, who had recently married Vanessa Redgrave – and so was now part of England's leading theatre dynasty – to direct Tallulah in a fairly immediate revival of *The Milk Train* in 1964.

The move was ill-advised. An ageing actor who looks a wreck may well turn out to be one, as was the case here. Perhaps the experience twenty years earlier of Laurette Taylor rising from the ashes of her career, overcoming her drink problem to give the performance of a lifetime in *The Glass Menagerie*, provided a misguided hope of something similar. In the event, the backstage atmosphere was poisonous, relations between director and star would have made a horror story of their own, the leading lady's performance failed to rise to expectations and the play, having limped from Baltimore to Broadway, expired in a welter of recriminations after only five performances.

The Milk Train Doesn't Stop Here Anymore was turned into a film called *Boom!* five years after the play's premiere, in 1968. The title came from what Chris gives as the name of his next work when Blackie asks him: 'Boom!' 'What does it mean?' she understandably replies, to which Chris says, just before drinking his wine as the curtain falls, 'It says "BOOM" and that's what it means: no translation, no explanation, just "BOOM".' Although it is one of his least-known films, *Boom!* provides a convenient moment to discuss Williams's on-screen work. As already mentioned, the many films that were made of his plays brought his writing to a far greater audience than would otherwise have been the case and that of *A Streetcar Named Desire* in particular gave him a cinematic immortality.

Translating from one medium to another is notoriously difficult, and admirers of novels and plays have often been disappointed with the transfer from page to screen. By the time *The Milk Train Doesn't Stop Here Anymore* became *Boom!*, over a dozen of Williams's plays had been filmed. It may be helpful to list them in release order here: *The Glass Menagerie* (1950), *A Streetcar Named Desire* (1951), *The Rose Tattoo* (1955), *Baby Doll* (1956), *Cat on a Hot Tin Roof* (1958), *Suddenly Last Summer* (1959), *The Fugitive Kind* – the film version of *Orpheus Descending* – (1960), *Summer and Smoke* (1961), *The Roman Spring of Mrs Stone* (1961), *Sweet Bird of Youth* (1962), *Period of Adjustment* (1962), *The Night of the Iguana* (1964) and *This Property is Condemned* (1966).

Williams's fame and the quality of his work attracted many leading lights of the cinema screen, including Katherine Hepburn (Mrs Venables in *Suddenly Last Summer*), Gertrude Lawrence (*The Glass Menagerie*), Burt Lancaster (*The Rose Tattoo*) and, also in *The Rose Tattoo*, one of Europe's biggest stars, the Italian actress Anna Magnani. Magnani was a close personal friend, and Tennessee greatly admired her zest for life, as well as her talent as an actress. He had written the part of Serafina Delle Rose for her, but her inadequate command of English made her appearance in the stage play impossible. She was, however, guaranteed the film part, in which she excelled, winning an Oscar for Best Actress.

Despite being associated with a raft of Oscars – *A Streetcar Named Desire* alone won four: best art direction/set direction, black and white; best actress (Vivien Leigh); best supporting actress (Kim Hunter as Stella); and best supporting actor (Karl Malden as Mitch) – Williams's relationship with the medium of film was less intense but often as troubled as that with the theatre. Film is very much more a director's medium, which is difficult for any writer. In Williams's case, any dissatisfaction with a movie, whether or not he had been involved in the screenplay (he was in only some of these) was doubly frustrating. He spent his life not just creating new work but adapting and tweaking it (although not necessarily for the better) and some- times, as with *The Two-character Play* in the late 1960s and through the 1970s, making several attempts – in different productions – at getting it right. With film, this revision was impossible.

In later years, after a few drinks, he would complain about the way Hollywood insisted on altering his plots for commercial reasons. He was very happy with the money that film rights brought in – Audrey Wood was adept at squeezing half a million dollars at a time out of producers – but sometimes despaired of the changes that were part of the price. These changes were partly dictated by the undeniable fact that film audiences, being made up of a less rarefied group than those in Broadway theatres, were not considered ready for some of the more boundary-pushing references to sex – specifically, gay sex – that Williams was able to make in playhouses. Hollywood's self-censoring was also informed by public pressure and the code by which the industry universally abided. This was to change in the course of the 1970s, but was still holding firm during the two decades when most of the films of his work were made.

The clearest example of a change to suit public taste was the ending of *Sweet Bird of Youth*. In the play, Chance is threatened with castration, the sight of which we are mercifully spared, but which, it

Tennessee with one of his favourite actresses, the Italian actress Anna Magnani, for whom he created the role of Rose in *The Rose Tattoo*, which won her an Academy Award.

is very clear, he will undergo moments after the curtain falls. In the film, Chance, played by Paul Newman (reprising his stage performance), suffers his punishment on-screen, but it has been drastically downgraded to only having his nose broken. This robs the punishment of its ferocity and its symbolism, as well as diluting the savagery of the thugs who carry it out.

Four years before his face was struck by a billiard cue in *Sweet Bird of Youth*, Paul Newman had played Brick in the film version of *Cat on a Hot Tin Roof*. Elia Kazan's insistence on a happier ending than Tennessee's original one when directing the play was all the more important for the film version. Paul Newman as Brick and Elizabeth Taylor as Maggie were at their astonishingly attractive physical peak at the time the film was made. It would have been incomprehensible to movie audiences for them *not* to come together in the end to produce an heir to Big Daddy's fortune, thus saving their marriage in the process. The homosexual aspect of Brick and Skipper's friendship was also changed, leaving only the slightest hint of it, for those who would or could read such subtext into the script.

Taylor would appear in other Tennessee Williams films, including *Suddenly Last Summer*, whose screenplay, by Gore Vidal, takes us onto the beach where Sebastian, the decadent gay poet, uses his cousin as bait for the boys he is after. Seeing Miss Taylor in a revealing white one-piece swimsuit with a plunging neckline, it is understandable that Sebastian is able to attract such a crowd. Williams was furious that Sebastian's death was shown rather than described, but if the action of a film is opened out – and it generally is given that film is such a visual medium – then audiences had to see the death.

Given this general principle, Elia Kazan had wanted to escape the stage set in his film version of *A Streetcar Named Desire*, and did so up to a point – for example, having Blanche and Stella go to the bowling alley where Stanley and his friends are enjoying an evening out – but the script made the return to, and focus on, the cramped flat in New Orleans' French quarter inevitable. Kazan did use something available to a film set rather than a stage though, reducing the size of the apartment as the action of the film progressed, increasing the sense of claustrophobia and sexual tension.

Marlon Brando played Stanley on-screen as well as on Broadway, and became a major star as a result. As already mentioned, Jessica Tandy was dropped in favour of the more bankable talent of Vivien Leigh, with whom audiences were very familiar as another Southern lady, Scarlett O'Hara from *Gone with the Wind*. Geraldine Page was luckier than Jessica Tandy, reprising her stage roles on film in both *Sweet Bird of Youth* and *Summer and Smoke*. No actor likes to be defined by one role but, though he was to be directed in another iconic part for Kazan, as the boxer Terry Malloy in *On the Waterfront*, Marlon Brando is forever associated with Stanley Kowalski. Cinema freezes actors at the point in their lives when they make films, immortalizing beauty. Though this creates a lasting record, it also holds an unforgiving and increasingly cruel reproach to them as they age. Brando's physical decline into thinning hair and obesity is all the more tragic for the glorious physical shape he flaunted in the film of *A Streetcar Named Desire*. Watching him in his third great role, that of Vito Corleone, the Mafia boss in *The Godfather*, it is impossible not to compare, with incredulity, the man one is watching (albeit made up to look older and with cotton wool inside his cheeks to fatten them out) with the force of sexual nature that he had been some twenty years earlier.

Age intruded in *Boom!*, which starred Elizabeth Taylor, by now a Williams veteran, and Richard Burton. Burton had been well cast as Lawrence Shannon in the film of *The Night of the Iguana,* a role that suited his worldly public persona at this stage. Because, by the late 1960s, he and Elizabeth Taylor were the most famous couple (as actors) in the world, it was deemed a commercial imperative to have them play opposite each other in *Boom!*, especially as the play it was based on was not an instantly recognizable classic and therefore needed some help in attracting the public's attention. The trouble was that Taylor was far too young to be playing Mrs Goforth, while Burton was much too old, heavy and rugged to play Chris Flanders. The film, therefore, was an unsurprising flop. What was a genuine surprise, and gives *Boom!* some residual interest, was the casting (unthinkable in the 1950s but amusingly with-it in 1968) of Noël Coward as The Witch of Capri. Coward and Tennessee knew each other socially and were, of course, aware of each other's work. Examining them as they were at this time, a few years before Coward's death in his beloved Jamaica, they make a telling contrast to each other. Coward was more of an all-round talent than Williams: he was a leading stage actor, a talented composer of both amusing light comedy numbers and achingly nostalgic melodies and a writer. However, like Williams he had been a hugely popular playwright (with his heyday before the war), had written the screenplay (adapted from a differently named one-act play) for what was to be one of the greatest screen weepies of all time, *Brief Encounter* (1945), and was, like Tennessee, an accomplished poet. Both men also shared a hobby as painters, each having a rather naive yet charming style on canvas.

By 1968 both men were physically well past their best – both were, in fact, to die in their early seventies – though Coward was a little more than eleven years older than Williams. Both men's plays had fallen out of fashion, as had Coward's musicals. This would make it all the more galling, in 1972, when Tennessee was told that his *Small Craft Warnings* was going to be pulled from the theatre it was playing at, to be replaced by a show called *Oh, Coward!*, in which two actors played Noël and his favourite leading lady, Gertrude Lawrence. Coward had had some success in this genre, most notably with *Bitter Sweet* (1929), but his musicals, like his plays, were considered wildly anachronistic by the start of the 1960s. The crucial difference between them at the time *Boom!* came out was that Coward had begun to enjoy a revival in his fortunes after more than a decade in the wilderness. The return to favour had begun four years earlier, when the National Theatre, under his old friend and acting colleague Sir Laurence Olivier, staged a new production of Coward's hit *Hay Fever* from the 1920s. With a starry cast that included Dame Edith Evans and two rising young actors, Maggie Smith and Derek Jacobi, *Hay Fever* launched what Coward self-deprecatingly called 'Dad's Renaissance'.

Although Williams was to be awarded a number of honours in the coming years, they were for past achievements and were never reflected in the critical or commercial reaction to his stream of new work. So it must have been vexing for him to watch as Coward's star rose once more – including as a film actor, giving a memorable cameo as a gangland boss lording it over everyone else in prison in the comedy thriller *The Italian Job* in 1969 – while his own continued to be dragged to earth. Coward, though older and unwell, had also managed a couple of years after he became fashionable again to appear in his own play, *A Song at Twilight*, in the West End, where he played a closeted gay man who, when outed by a female ex-lover, makes a speech about how the English public are not yet ready to accept homosexuality. Though tame by today's standards, it was a daring step for a man who had always, to his public if not his friends, been firmly in the closet.

Coward's plays, with the exception of *Still Life* (which became *Brief Encounter*) and *Blithe Spirit*, did not really lend themselves to cinema. Did Williams's plays? Yes, up to a point. Many were successfully filmed and the fact that his plays were all relatively domestic – even if like *Boom!* the setting is dramatic, on a cliff above the Mediterranean – made them relatively inexpensive to make. They were also attractive to actors as the roles they were cast in were already, thanks to the success of the stage plays, well known as star vehicles, as well as coming with a certain artistic validity. Playing a major Williams role was as much an endorsement of an actor's status as being cast in a major Chekhov or Shakespeare.

This explains why his works attracted film finance and stellar casts. They also tended to make money. But his heart was in the theatre. This showed in his work, which, being focused on individuals and the conflicts in their lives, was better adapted to the intensity of the stage than the expansive opportunities of the screen. True, he had grown up with cinema and, through non-naturalistic sets and skilful use of lighting and music, his plays had the fluidity that was one of cinema's main attractions. However, with the exception of *A Streetcar Named Desire*, his work is always best seen on stage rather than on the screen and benefits hugely from the unspoken yet electrically charged interaction between actors and audience in a shared space. The original medium of choice, a book, is also where *The Roman Spring of Mrs Stone* works best. It is a tribute to his talent that his stories were seized with relish by the film world; however, to experience their full flavour, they should be seen in the theatre.

Returning to his stage career, Tennessee's next theatrical opening, in 1966, was a double bill. Collectively called *Slapstick Tragedy*, and opening at the Longacre Theatre in New York, the two plays that made up the evening were *The Mutilated* and *The Gnadiges Fraulein*. *The Mutilated* is a black comedy centred on two women, both damaged outcasts: Trinket is a wealthy eccentric who has had one breast removed after suffering from cancer, while Celeste is a thief, recently released from prison. Other characters include Maxie, who operates a sort of freak show with Bird Girl, a deformed woman whose nickname, like that of the Elephant Man, suggests the extent and type of her deformity. The play has a Greek chorus, the Carollers, who sing songs relevant to the action and theme of each scene. A mysterious figure, Jack in Black, dressed in a diamond-encrusted black cowboy outfit, is a symbol of death. He appears as a result of Trinket feeling fresh pain in her chest and fearing it is a sign of the return of cancer. Her impending death is, however, averted by an appearance by the Virgin Mary, who banishes the pain and protects the women from Jack.

The second play, *The Gnadiges Fraulein*, is a bizarre, surreal play with more than a hint of a bad dream about it. The Fraulein in question is a blind-in-one-eye woman who has been attacked by the Cocaloony bird, a huge nightmarish creature she had fought with in order to get her hands on the catch landed at the docks by fishermen. In the course of the play the Fraulein, who has, earlier in her life, been on the stage, is attacked once again and blinded in the other eye. We learn her back story: she was in a circus where she developed a performance trick – grabbing fish from a trainer before a seal could get to it – that so enraged the animal involved that it knocked all her teeth out! Though the image at the end of the play is of the indomitable Fraulein setting off to the docks to get more fish, despite the horror of her handicap, this is a play – very much in the tradition of the theatre of the absurd – that is a curiosity, not a classic. However interesting it is as an example of its genre (and Tennessee's works are invariably interesting, even when less than brilliant), *The Gnadiges Fraulein* was a gift to critics who berated the playwright for not producing work like *A Streetcar Named Desire* or *Cat on a Hot Tin Roof* any more.

Two years on, in March 1968, in the later part of 'the stoned age' spent mourning Frank Merlo through tumblers of whisky and bottles of prescription drugs, Williams had a full-length play, written the previous year, open in New York at the Ethel Barrymore Theatre. Originally called *The Kingdom of Earth*, it was renamed *The Seven Descents of Myrtle*, which is a much more 1960s-sounding title. A seven-scene play, *The Seven Descents of Myrtle* was developed from an earlier one-act piece set on a farm in the Mississippi Delta. It deals with themes of inheritance, death and sex. The three central characters are Chicken, his half-brother Lot and Lot's new wife, Myrtle. Lot, who is dying of tuberculosis, returns to the family farm, which he owns but which is run by Chicken. Chicken's mother, of mixed race, was their father's mistress before he married Lot's mother.

Myrtle was unaware that her husband had a brother, or that he was dying, when she married him. Against a background of danger – there is a Delta flood due at any moment – the sexual tension in the house increases, with Chicken's overt, virile masculinity ever more contrasted with Lot's blood-spattered coughing fits. Chicken makes it clear that he wants to inherit the family farm, and persuades Myrtle to write a document waiving her right to inherit. Lot, it transpires, is not only tubercular, he is also a transvestite with a mother fetish. After Chicken and Myrtle have had sex, Lot emerges from the first-floor bedroom, descending the stairs in his mother's white evening gown. After he collapses, Chicken asks Myrtle to stay with him and have children. She reveals she has already given birth to several who were adopted because she could not afford to keep them.

The play was poorly reviewed and lasted fewer than thirty performances on Broadway before closing. Much of the criticism was that it featured many of Williams's usual themes, which had been far better expressed in earlier work – specifically, *A Streetcar Named Desire*. Lot was seen as a male version of Blanche DuBois (ironic, given the occasional allegation that Blanche is, essentially, a man in drag), while Chicken was very much a Stanley Kowalski figure, with Myrtle resembling Stella. The comparisons are valid: both plays also have a dispute about inherited property. However, *The Seven Descents of Myrtle*, years before it became a one-act play, was originally a short story. Written in 1942, it pre-dated *A Streetcar Named Desire* by five years.

As with the contrasting popularity of the original productions of *The Glass Menagerie* and *Summer and Smoke*, this was a case of the better play (*Streetcar*) having being performed first. *The Seven Descents of Myrtle/Kingdom of Earth* is not a bad work: the themes are universal ones placed in a specific and very atmospheric rural Southern context and, unlike in *A Streetcar Named Desire*, the male character is essentially sympathetic. Chicken's victory over Lot and his inheritance of the farm – and Lot's wife – makes practical sense. He is in every way the man best suited to look after the land and populate it with his own children. Lot's unsuitability as patriarch is telegraphed not just by his illness and impotence but by his penchant for wearing drag, transforming himself into a younger version of his deceased mother in a rather sinister way that calls to mind Norman Bates in *Psycho*. Even creepier is his admission to Myrtle that his facility for make-up, and even dying his hair, was taught to him by his mother. It was she who said that, with his fair skin and blue eyes, he would look far prettier as a blond than a brunette.

In Williams's work, the link between drag and gay culture is a strong one. True, there are many references to hunky young hustlers, but the stereotype of gay as wannabe-woman, or having to dress as a female to attract straight males, occurs several times. This is partly a reflection of a regular sub-section of mainstream gay life at the time and partly the obvious potential it has, for a writer who likes melodrama, for a touch of the grotesque, and of the sad. For, despite the energy and humour of many drag acts, there is something essentially melancholic about them, as there is, on one level, in *any* theatrical performance: however larger-than-life the character onstage seems to be, the reality behind it is someone who, as the wig, dress and make-up come off, is entirely different from the brash, in-your-face persona they transform themselves into, and as they remove each layer of make-believe their vulnerability becomes steadily more evident.

It was the sadness rather than the onstage joie de vivre that Tennessee focused on in his short play *And Tell Sad Stories of the Death of Queens.* The title is a reference to Richard II's speech, in Shakespeare's history play, where he talks of telling sad stories of the death of kings. First performed at the Kennedy Center, Washington, DC, in 2004, decades after he wrote it, *And Tell Sad Stories of the Death*

A scene from a production of *The Kingdom of Earth* at the Print Room Theatre, 2011, a relatively new London venue and an example of the way Tennessee's lesser-known work continues to be explored by contemporary theatre companies.

of Queens is set during Mardi Gras, in the French quarter of New Orleans. Candy is an effeminate 35-year-old gay man (an interior designer as well, so all the stereotypes are being rolled out here), who had been in a long-term relationship. His partner, an older man, has left him for someone younger, so Candy, desperate for company as much as for sex, picks up a sailor and brings him home. Though the bar they meet in is one for gay men, the sailor claims that he is straight and wants a woman, not a man – however pretty.

Because Candy has his own business, he can afford to pay for casual sex but what he wants is a long-term relationship, and he is prepared to fund this, too. As he makes a very attractive 'woman', he hopes the sailor, Karl, will come to an accommodation with him. It is screamingly obvious that Karl is entirely the wrong sort to try to have a relationship with, but that is the very reason Candy is so attracted to him – very much a case of Quentin Crisp's belief that effeminate gay men (of his generation, at least) were attracted to manifestly masculine men who, by definition, would never want any sort of relationship with them. Williams unobtrusively makes Candy so sympathetic – he is the latest in a long line of delicate moths drawn to the flame – that one wants to leap onto the stage and urge him to find someone else. It was precisely this emotional impact of the dramatist's art that drew Williams away from poetry and into the theatre. Determined to get his man, Candy goes overboard with his preparations. He decides to get rid of the young men, who are also gay, who rent the apartment above his (he owns the whole house) in case they interfere with what he sees as the impending romance with his sailor. Karl turns out to be nothing more than a violent thug who beats and robs Candy, leaving him broken-hearted to be comforted by the young neighbours he had been planning to evict. *And Tell Sad Stories of the Death of Queens* suggests that any attempt to have a relationship with a macho straight man is doomed and that gay men should stick with each other.

A more nuanced drama, this time a short story rather than a play, is *The Killer Chicken and the Closet Queen.* This was written in 1977 and published in 1978. In the story, Stephen, a successful late thirty-something lawyer who is a closet homosexual, has a dilemma. His very wealthy mother, from whom he will eventually inherit a vast amount of money, is coming for lunch, along with partners in his law firm and their wives, but he has fobbed off his mother – for fifteen years – with stories of a non-existent love affair with a woman called Sue Coffin. This is a dig at Tennessee's father, using the middle name that was given to him as reference to relatives who were among the first Europeans to settle in Nantucket.

While panicking about this seemingly impossible feat, Stephen is simultaneously asked to take in – to live with him – the beautiful teenage younger brother of the young wife of the oldest of the partners in the law firm. She brings the boy, Clove, with her to Stephen's apartment well before the others arrive for the grand lunch. Stephen, who is already hung over, is stunned by the boy's beauty. The boy gets him drunk and has sex with him. Stephen emerges from his room a whole hour later to find an appalled gathering of guests about to leave. He loses his job. Stephen's mother, who comes round much later in the day, is persuaded by Clove (the idea was Stephen's) that he is Stephen's love child by Sue Coffin, who, he lies, died in childbirth and therefore cannot be presented to her. On a train journey down to Palm Beach to visit Stephen's mother, Clove makes it clear that he's going to arrange her death so they can have the use of her fortune.

Williams's fortune, in the sense of luck rather than money – productions of his earlier plays continued to bring in royalties – showed no signs of rallying, and this latest failure added to his ill health and the paranoia that had long been one of his less endearing qualities. In January 1969 his brother, Dakin, who had become a Roman Catholic as a young man, tried a radically different approach to combatting this decline and somehow persuaded him to see a Catholic priest. Williams did, and converted to Rome. He was received into the faith in Key West, in a church with the wonderfully poetic (and very Tennessee Williams) name of St Mary Star of the Sea.

Unlike Evelyn Waugh, who had grasped at the pre-Vatican II orthodoxies of Roman Catholicism as a protection from an unstable and threatening world, Williams was attracted to the church's theatricality rather than its theology. True, he made yet another trip to Rome, soon after his conversion, and was introduced to the head of the Jesuit order, but he seems to have had little interest in the religion itself. For him the wafer at communion was, in a sense, just another pill with which to cope with life. His conversion, which by definition linked him more closely with Christianity at the time, was perhaps a way of reconnecting with and affirming the importance of his relationship with his late grandfather. Though the Reverend Walter Dakin had been an Episcopalian priest, that branch of Christianity shared with the Roman Catholics an enjoyment of ceremony in worship. It was the fact of entering a church that mattered to Williams, not the denomination.

That Tennessee continued to be troubled despite the potential consolations of religion was, as ever, expressed through his work, to which he continued to devote whatever resources he could muster. His next play was *In the Bar of a Tokyo Hotel*, which opened in May 1969 at the Eastside Playhouse, New York. Set in Japan, where a famous American painter, Mark, and his wife, Miriam, are staying, the play features a portrait of an ageing artist suffering from alcoholism, sexual problems and a general anxiety bordering on madness. There has been some debate as to whether this is meant to be autobiographical or whether the artist is actually a portrait of his friend Jackson Pollock, who had died back in 1956.

If it was based on Pollock's life and his troubled marriage to fellow artist Lee Krasner, the character who most represents the playwright is Leonard, the art dealer who sells Mark's work and who is summoned to Japan by Miriam, who wants her husband, now a physical and mental wreck, to be hospitalized back in the United States. The resentment that Miriam shows towards Leonard (who is gay) and her suspicion that he may have a more than commercial and friendly interest in her husband, mirrors the edginess that Lee Krasner showed towards Williams's friendship with Jackson Pollock. On the other hand, Miriam and Mark openly suggest, in the middle of a vicious marital argument in which Mark hurls recriminations at Miriam for her promiscuity, that the pair of them are somehow two sides of the same personality.

Miriam is a well-drawn (no pun intended) character whose sophistication and unapologetic sensuality have more than a touch of *The Graduate*'s Mrs Robinson. She brings a dry wit to the play and her quips and innuendo – and inappropriate advances – with the young Japanese barman are very enjoyable. Miriam has her neuroses too. She takes an irrational dislike to inanimate objects, especially flowers, and she lacks any real sympathy with her husband's ill health, but there is something vital about her dry humour, her desire to explore, to enjoy life and to move forwards. She would certainly recognize and echo Tennessee's war cry of 'En avant!' She makes it clear that when Death comes for her, he'll have a fight on his hands: 'I know it would have to remove, wrench, tear! – the bracelets off my arms. Insignia of attraction still persisting . . .'

Most reviews were negative. The critic for the *New York Times* wrote, 'Mr Williams has never perhaps been over-reluctant to show the world his wounds – but in this new play he seems to be doing nothing else.' Though the reviewer had a point, this was rather unfair. The play might be criticized for its brevity – the relationship between artist and gallery-owner could have been explored more – but it is more than just a playwright's whinge about the difficulty of creating art. In terms of creation, what Williams was writing about in *In the Bar of a Tokyo Hotel* was the exhaustion induced by creating a new *type* of art. Mark had been very successful as a traditional

Tennessee Williams with Andy Warhol – a representative of a new generation of American artists. Warhol's star was rising while Tennessee's was fading, but the playwright was still widely admired and seen as a social catch at any party.

painter – Miriam has hundreds of his early works in storage; they are worth a fortune and will fund her impending widowhood. It is his new, ultra-modernist work that takes so much out of him and which both Miriam and Leonard think will be unsellable to a public who are used to his more conventional art. The parallels with the playwright's own career are strikingly obvious. It is ironic that it seems to have passed by many critics, who once again complained of his new style of writing and attacked him for it.

His response was, as ever, to sail away – this time to Japan. This was not a defiant gesture, given the setting of his latest work, but a trip to see a Japanese production of *A Streetcar Named Desire*. Another example of the public preferring his classic work, his frustrations came out in the usual way and he was, on this visit, in almost as terrible a physical state as the painter Mark had been in the play. Unlike Mark, Williams survived Japan and returned to America, where he travelled between San Francisco, New York, New Orleans and Key West. It was when he was in Key West that his mental health gave such cause for concern that Dakin, having tried religion to help his brother at the beginning of the year, now insisted on hospitalization. Tennessee had badly burned himself while trying to make a meal, and this was the trigger for immediate action. Dakin had him confined to the mental ward of a hospital in St Louis and though his brother hated him for it – confinement in a mental home, as had happened to Rose, being Tennessee's greatest fear – this saved his life. Whether that was, ultimately, kind, is a matter for debate, but it did give Williams another fourteen years in which to write. These were years which saw further embittering rejections by the theatre establishment, but which produced several plays that, in the twenty-first century, have been successfully revived and improved his reputation as a playwright.

5

The 1970s: Small Craft Warnings

As the 1970s began, Tennessee Williams had been offered another chance at life and at writing – which for him were one and the same thing. The coming ten years, the last full decade of his life, were to prove even more troubled than the previous ten, as his physical health and his reputation continued to free fall. Despite this, muttering 'En avant!', he continued to create new plays and was to publish his memoirs.

He also made a very rare foray into politics, appearing at a rally at the Cathedral of St John the Divine in New York to protest against the Vietnam War. He was persuaded to do so by a close friend of his, Dotson Rader. A much younger man, a writer who was politically active, he encouraged Tennessee to take part. More characteristically, Tennessee wrote a poem on the campaign's behalf, the publication fee for which he gave to the cause, along with that of an article, 'We Are Dissenters Now', that was published in *Harper's Bazaar*. His duty done, he turned back to his plays. Of these, one of the best was *Small Craft Warnings*, which opened at the Truck and Warehouse Theater in New York in April 1972. As usual, it was based on earlier writing, a one-act play of the previous year called *Confessional*. Set in a bar on the southern California coast, its characters address the audience directly, in a spotlit section of the play whose lighting zone suggests a confessional box.

Typically about a disparate group of people's loneliness and longing for love, it includes a handsome drifter (Bobby), a middle-aged queen (Quentin) and two rival women, Leona and Violet. Despite her potential for violence, Leona is a sympathetic, larger-than-life character, middle-aged yet still sexually charged, looking for companionship and offering it to young Bobby, who reminds her of her dead gay brother. The difficulty of finding a satisfying relationship is typified by Quentin, who, having picked up Bobby, rejects the idea of sex with him – because Bobby is gay! Quentin is only excited by straight men. The straight men on offer in the bar are virulently anti-gay and in any case an unappealing bunch. Among them is the disreputable figure of Doc, a medic who has lost his licence and is run out of town when a birth he leaves the bar to attend goes horribly wrong: the child is stillborn and the mother dies of blood loss. Tennessee played the role of Doc for some of the play's moderately successful run, in a rather desperate attempt to attract audiences.

The following year, 1973, saw the latest outing of *The Two-character Play*. This play had been staged in London back in 1967 at the Hampstead Theatre, where despite having fashionable actors of the time, Mary Ure and Peter Wyngarde, it was a failure. The play, revised and retitled as *Out Cry*, was next performed at the Ivanhoe Theatre in Chicago four years later, before being staged at the Lyceum in New York, still called *Out Cry*, where it ran for less than two weeks. A fourth version, as *The Two-character Play*, was once more staged in New York, this time at the Quaigh Theatre, in August 1975 and a fifth was put on at the Showcase Theatre in San Francisco, where Williams was to meet Lyle Leverich, his future biographer.

The play, under both its names, was dear to Williams's heart, though others have been less certain of its merits. The epitome of the experimental, avant-garde work that he turned to in the 1960s and 1970s, and which was so comprehensively rejected at the time, its first version had been written as he hurtled towards nervous collapse. As its name implies, it has just two characters, a brother, Felice, and sister, Clare, who are actors and managers of their own touring theatre company. They have, in their repertoire, a play called *The Two-character Play*, so the work is a play-within-a-play with elements of a play within that, too.

Felice, a stylish but camp figure and Clare, who has serious psychological problems (yet another shade of Rose), are in a rundown small-town theatre in the back of beyond – 'a state theatre in an unknown state'. An enervating combination of manically paced touring, self-absorption, an inherent lack of practicality and drug-induced mental instability finds them onstage but unsure of where exactly (in which theatre) they are. Hearing the murmur of the audience in front of the curtain (the actual audience watching this play), they are alone on their side of the proscenium arch as the rest of the company, even down to the stage manager, have left them, tired of working without pay for a couple who they dismiss as 'insane'.

In a warped nod to the theatrical tradition of 'the show must go on', they decide to perform *The Two-character Play* for the audience, though in doing so their current disputes and crises break through. Tempted to shoot each other with a (real) revolver onstage, neither has the guts to do so. They are left in a state of collapse, locked in an empty theatre from which Felice has already found there is no escape. The obvious exit – through the auditorium in which the audience, for whom they have been performing, is sitting – seems not to be open to them, suggesting that their belief in the audience's presence was a desperate delusion. Their doom is summed up in the playwright's final stage directions:

Felice raises his eyes to watch the light fade from the face of his sister as it is fading from his: in both their faces is a tender admission of defeat. They reach out their hands to one another, and the light lingers a moment on their hands slowly lifting toward each other. As they slowly embrace, there is total dark, in which the curtain falls.

When *Out Cry* was staged in New York in 1973, it starred Michael York, a popular actor best known for his film roles (including Brian in *Cabaret* and Tybalt in Franco Zeffirelli's much-admired screen version of *Romeo and Juliet*). Despite his box-office wattage, the play flopped, and Tennessee had wailed, in a letter to his friend Maria St Just – whose relationship with Tennessee is discussed further in Chapter Seven – that 'You don't recover from a failure like *Out*

Audrey Wood, the agent whose foresight and support launched and sustained Tennessee's career until their final falling out.

Cry.' His determination to try to do just that, stubborn or heroic according to taste, saw him continue to produce new work.

That work was no longer represented by Audrey Wood, Williams's agent since 1939, the woman who had done more than anyone else (with Elia Kazan a close second) to nurture his talent and promote his plays. She fell victim to his paranoia, to a personality trait that saw him, at his most hysterical, turn on old friends, accusing them of betrayal. At those moments, the genial, affectionate side of his personality which earned him, along with his talent, so many friends in the first place, was swept aside by a malevolent and self-destructive rage against an insult or offence that had not taken place nor ever existed. It was in Chicago in 1971, prior to the opening of *Out Cry* there, that the break occurred. The production was not going well. Tennessee was hugely stressed by this, and, looking for someone to blame for what threatened to be yet another frustrating disappointment, he attacked Audrey Wood for not giving him or the play the level of support a major playwright should expect from his agent. In a fit of rage, he sacked her. Though she was replaced by another agent from the company that Wood had latterly worked with (ICM, or International Creative Management, one of the leading companies of its type in the world), the magic circle that she had spun around him was broken; an essential prop to his creative life had been kicked, by him, from under him – another casualty of his continued mental decline.

The first of the post-Wood plays to be performed was *The Red Devil Battery Sign*. This had been started four years earlier, and optioned by the producer David Merrick in 1973, but it did not open until June 1976, at the Shubert Theatre in Boston. Set in Dallas in the aftermath of the Kennedy assassination and featuring a very 1960s sense of political corruption, conspiracy theories and left-wing revolution, the background gives it more in common with his earliest plays and their backdrop of social and economic crisis than the personal dramas of the 1940s and 1950s or the black comedies of his final years.

The central character, who has no name, just the appellation of the Woman Downtown, is a wealthy one-time socialite brought up in a political household, who then married a businessman. Possessing secret papers that reveal a conspiracy concerning the Vietnam War, she had been confined to a mental institution and subjected to long-term electric shock therapy. Now living, anonymously, in a smart hotel, with a bodyguard who she also feels is something of a jailer – a similar attitude to Princess Diana's towards the police – she meets and falls in love with King Del Rey, a Mexican band leader who is dying of a brain tumour. The two have an affair, while King's daughter, a singer who has fallen for an unsuitable computer nerd, is gradually reconciled with her father. The Woman Downtown complains of corporate forces, the red devils whose battery sign's light sweeps across the neighbouring streets in an intrusive and possessive way. Eventually King dies, and the Woman, throwing off all the trappings of a society she loathes, joins a group of urban delinquents, becoming a mother figure to these 'wolves'.

Williams claimed that *The Red Devil Battery Sign* was a response to President Kennedy's assassination, which itself was the subject of numerous conspiracy theories, many linked to Kennedy's predecessor's – President Eisenhower's – warning about the growing influence of the 'military industrial complex'. The play addresses the issue of racial discrimination – a very topical one in America through the 1960s and beyond – in the form of King Del Rey, who has tried all his life to avoid being anything like the American caricature of a Mexican. The play's essential message is the importance of human connection in an increasingly impersonal technology-driven society, a message that gives it a topical relevance, for all its highly stylized and very Californian setting.

In 1975 Williams published his memoirs. Highly entertaining and, as one would expect, vividly written, they caused a shock by their frankness in describing his sex life. He had created a minor sensation when interviewed on David Frost's TV show at the very start of the decade, in January 1970. During the interview he, in effect, came out, saying of his range of sexual experiences, 'I covered the waterfront!' In his memoirs he went into explicit detail about what happened on those nightly expeditions. He did at least have the grace to use pseudonyms when describing some of his sexual partners, but pulled no punches when it came to his family, dismissing his mother as 'a moderately controlled hysteric'.

The book would have caused a stir even if he had been an up-and-coming young rebel. Yet by this stage he had been awarded a doctorate of humanities by the University of Missouri and had also received the Gold Medal for Drama from the American Academy of Arts and Letters, both in 1969. In 1975 he was awarded the Medal of Honour for Literature from the National Arts Club, and in 1976 he was to be elected to the American Academy of Arts and Letters. The contrast between these accolades from august institutions and his rackety personal life was striking. The awards may have recognized his past but they were unable to influence the present. The year 1977 was to see his next theatrical failure. The remorselessness of these reverses is depressing enough to *read* about, years after the event. No wonder it had such a cumulatively damaging effect on him at the time. It may also explain why he was reluctant to talk about his work with other people, even at awards events. At one such event, for example, he was furious when questioned about his writing over the lunch table and created a scene. Though he lived for his work, he hated talking about it to anyone except his friends.

On the one hand this was a reflection of his touchiness: his later plays had been so conspicuously unsuccessful that he was wary of any conversation about his craft – even hits like *Streetcar*. No artist likes talking about their failures, and Williams seems to have felt edgy about the possibility of any discussion moving on to less happy terrain. On the other hand, he was basically a shy man who preferred the company of friends to that of strangers, however distinguished or flattering they may have been. This shyness was masked by his sometimes over-the-top public behaviour, tipping over into drunken excess and hysterical scenes, but this unattractive side to him was born from a deep-seated insecurity rather than inherent bad manners or egotism. It could be argued that it was also another aspect of what he had, years earlier, memorably referred to as 'the catastrophe of success'. Once success and the fame and fortune that go with it has been achieved, anything less than a triumph can be deeply wounding: a sign that the longed-for position could at any moment slip from one's grasp.

A lot of artists fit this category and their occasional bad behaviour can be explained by it. What makes Tennessee Williams so sympathetic, despite the scale of his tantrums when he felt his friendship had been betrayed or his artistry undermined (both at once in the case of his falling out with Audrey Wood), is that all he really cared about was his writing. The insecurity and the problems that it brought were not because he loved money or position and wanted to cling to them, but because he cared, desperately, about the value of his work. Because he lived so much for and through it, discussing it as part of polite conversation with someone at a society lunch or awards ceremony was, for him, akin to being expected to open his most private feelings and fears to a stranger.

The next piece he placed before a critical firing squad was a memory play, *Vieux Carré*, set in the French quarter of New Orleans, from which the work got its title. It lasted only five performances in New York, although it fared better the next year at the Nottingham Playhouse in England and at the Piccadilly Theatre in London in 1979. That it is highly autobiographical, with the central character of the young writer explicitly modelled on the playwright himself, is stated in his notes setting the scene of the play, where he refers to the writer as 'myself those many years ago'. Intriguingly, more modern research has suggested that elements of the play may have been worked on while Tennessee was still living in New Orleans, in early 1939. These elements were expanded in a shorter play, *I Never Get Dressed Till After Dark on a Sunday*, before finally ending up as *Vieux Carré*.

The play describes the experiences of The Writer in a wildly eccentric boarding house in the French Quarter, where a motley collection of lodgers lives in small rooms or cubicles with wafer-thin partitions. In some ways it is a modern-day version of *La Bohème*, but without the jolly student camaraderie of Puccini's opera. One of The Writer's neighbours, an artist, has the very operatic (*La Bohème* again, and indeed *La traviata*) ailment of tuberculosis, which he refuses to accept. We later realize that another lodger, Jane, also suffers from the same disease. In remission, she has had an affair with a stock Tennessee character – a beautiful, well-built, unreliable and narcissistic youth called Tye. After they have made love and he is preparing to leave for work, Jane expresses her bitterness at her illness and the inevitable effect it has on any chance of lasting love:

> What's understandable is that your present convenience is about to become an encumbrance. An invalid, of no use, financial or sexual. Sickness is repellent, Tye, demands more care and gives less and less in return. The person you loved – assuming that you did love when she was still useful – is now, is now as absorbed in preparing herself for oblivion as you were absorbed, in your – your image in the – mirror!

The year 1978 produced *Tiger Tail*, which is the only example of Williams turning a screenplay (*Baby Doll*) into a play – normally the adaptation process worked the other way round. *Tiger Tail* was performed at the Alliance Theatre in Atlanta, Georgia. It lacked the scandalous appeal that *Baby Doll* had had twenty years – and a moral lifetime – earlier, but it was a skilful stage adaptation of a film, a hard act to carry off.

The King's Head Theatre (London) production in 2012 of *Vieux Carré*, Tennessee's memory play of his early days in New Orleans.

January 1979 saw his latest play, a comedy, open in New York at the Hudson Guild Theatre, after a promising try-out in South Carolina. A four-hander (with other voices offstage), *A Lovely Sunday for Creve Coeur* is set in the 1930s, in what was then called an 'efficiency apartment'. Small and excruciatingly decorated, with glaringly bright and horribly clashing colours, the apartment is shared by Dorothea ('Dotty') and Bodey. Dotty is attractive, though not as young as she was, and in danger of being left on the shelf from which Bodey never stood a chance of descending. A dumpy early-middle-aged German-American, Bodey, we learn, has been waging a long-term campaign to pair Dotty off with Bodey's equally unprepossessing twin brother. As the play opens, Dotty, who is a teacher of civics, is performing exhausting physical exercise to keep herself trim and beguiling. She is waiting, increasingly desperately, for a phone call from her lover, Ralph Ellis. Ralph, with whom she has had sex, turns out to be a well-born young man who, despite moving in the best social circles, is the principal of the school where Dotty works.

The apartment has two visitors in the course of the play. Sophie Gluck, from upstairs, is another German-American spinster, older than Bodey. Though the playwright gets laughs from Bodey's Teutonic background, which is shared with Tennessee Williams's much-loved grandmother, she is sympathetically drawn, unlike Miss Gluck, who is a grotesque character. Miss Gluck barely speaks English, is desperately lonely and is a figure of fun, from the way a door is slammed in her face when she first appears, to the diarrhoea she always suffers from after one of Bodey's cups of coffee.

Admittedly a minor play, *A Lovely Sunday for Creve Coeur* works well as a comedy, and if it has a message as such, it is that one should beware of the beautiful – they make the rules. Dotty has a rule of her own – 'I've always drawn a strict line with a man' – but handsome young Ralph blithely ignores it, and seduces her in his expensive car. His looks trump her morals, while in the course of the play, we learn that he has very few scruples of his own. The piece suggests that companionship and kindness – for all her eccentricities, Bodey is genuinely kind towards Sophie and has Dotty's best interests at heart – are what matter most. This is an older man's view of life, treating passion as a dangerous delusion, but it makes the point without being in any way preachy.

The inevitable autobiographical content comes in the form of the setting – St Louis, which is not portrayed in a flattering light – and in Bodey's job, which is at the International Shoe Company, where Tennessee and his father had both worked. Williams also gives Dotty a romantic back story, of having gone out with a young musical prodigy who suffered from premature ejaculation of the most dramatic kind:

> I'd feel him plunging, plunging against me that – that – frantic part of him . . . then he'd release me at once and collapse on the

porch swing, breathing hoarsely. With the corner gas lamp shining through the wisteria vines, it was impossible not to notice the wet stain spreading on his light flannel trousers.

Tennessee had suffered from the same problem, with girls, as a young man. His first romantic interest, at school, had been a girl called Hazel Kramer and with her he had made a fool of himself in the same way that the musical prodigy had with Dotty. Tennessee had been dancing with Hazel on a riverboat, a highly romantic situation which was ruined by what happened next, as he recalled in his *Memoirs*: 'She wore a pale green chiffon party dress with no sleeves and we went up on the dark upper deck and I put my arm about those delicious shoulders and I "came" in my white flannels.' Here he exorcizes the memory of it through humour. Dotty visits the family doctor to discuss her young man's embarrassing problem. The doctor is archly amused rather than sympathetic, laconically observing '[he] must have a large laundry bill'.

The other character, also female, is Helena Brookmire, an elegantly dressed woman with a ready way with sarcasm. One can imagine her being played by Coral Browne, in the style of Mercy Croft, the character she portrayed in the film of *The Killing of Sister George*. Helena considers herself many cuts above Bodey on the social scale, which to be fair she is, but it also transpires that her friendship with Dotty is a self-interested one – she sees Dotty as a useful way of defraying her own expenses. Helena has called round, on a Sunday, to try to get a cheque out of Dotty towards the smart apartment she has persuaded her to join her in renting. Not content with that, she also tries to tap Dotty for money towards a car. We are alerted to Helena's lack of real decency by Williams's typical use of bird imagery. She is told by Bodey, 'You got eyes like a bird and I don't mean a songbird.' Bodey also rounds on Helena when the latter refers to herself as civilized: 'Stylish, yes, civilized no, unless a hawk or a buzzard is a civilized creature.' At this time in his life, Williams dismissed many of the young men who flitted in and out of his orbit as 'con men'. The bitterness at those whom he felt had ulterior motives for wanting to share his life comes out in the gradual revelation of Helena as someone whose interest in living with Dotty is entirely mercenary.

Going back to the bird theme, Bodey has a name that sounds remarkably like Birdy. Though her 'nest' is gaudy, with clashing colours and tasteless patterns, she is very much a mother hen, happily cooking for Dotty as well as for herself, putting together food for the Sunday picnics that, like a mother, she arranges. In a similarly maternal fashion, she also makes sure that Dotty has the essentials, like shampoo, and worries over Dotty's immature crush on the handsome Ralph Ellis. During the action, Helena and Bodey are aware, as Dotty is not until the end of the play, that Ralph has just been using her for some premarital fun. His engagement to a more socially suitable girl – described in the stage directions as 'a young woman, good looking in a plain fashion, wearing a hard smile of triumph' – is in the newspaper that Bodey tries, unsuccessfully, to hide from Dotty. Her dream of romance and a better future suddenly over, Dotty refuses to move in with Helena and, having spent much of the play insisting she isn't interested in Bodey's brother (alliteratively called Buddy) or in carrying on the regular Sunday routine of a picnic at the Creve Coeur park, she now decides that she will join them after all. The possibility is left hanging that perhaps Dotty will fulfil Bodey's dearest hope and settle down with the dull but dependable Buddy.

Tennessee's private life in the 1970s was anything but dull and dependable. He mixed casual sex, often with hustlers, with longer-term arrangements but none of these seems to have been particularly peaceful – far from it. The presence of so much drama – of rows, tantrums, scenes in public – suggests that though he wanted companionship, if not love, and the gentleness and support that comes with it, he was attracted (as he had been since his relationship with Pancho) to the drama of distinctly more tempestuous affairs. Little wonder he sympathized with moths drawn to flame.

One relationship that was very important to him was with a young ex-Vietnam veteran, Robert Carroll. Blond, blue-eyed and good-looking, he and Williams were together, on and off, for several years, and even after the final split came they remained on basically good terms. Tennessee's painting of him, naked except for a dressing gown which is open to reveal his torso, upper legs and genitals, was on the cover of his second volume of poetry, *Androgyne, Mon Amour*, published in 1977. Though he complained about Carroll to friends on occasion, he seems to have had an almost paternal sense of responsibility for him. Or perhaps a better analogy would be that of a much older brother looking out for a sometimes wayward younger sibling. As his relationship with his real-life kid brother, Dakin, had never been particularly close and was damaged beyond repair by the incarceration in the mental wing of Barnes Hospital, St Louis in 1969, Robert Carroll would certainly have provided an attractive filling for this emotional gap in Tennessee's life. That this part of his attraction to the much younger man was in some way fraternal is validated by the fact that, after providing for his sister Rose's financial needs, Carroll was the only individual left a regular lifetime income in Tennessee's will – as if he, too, was a much-loved part of Tennessee's family.

6

The 1980s: Steps Must Be Gentle

In 1980 Williams followed the wisecracks and bitchy repartee of *A Lovely Sunday for Creve Coeur* with something that is a dramatic reading rather than a play. His mother, Edwina, died that year after a long illness, aged 95, and it is unlikely to be a coincidence that this new piece, *Steps Must Be Gentle*, and a later work – his last, new, full-length play to be performed in his lifetime – both had mother/son relationships at their cores.

In *Steps Must Be Gentle* (a title taken from one of Hart Crane's best poems, 'My Grandmother's Love Letters'), the performers represent the poet and his mother, Grace Hart Crane. The piece is both a product of Tennessee's lifelong devotion to Crane's poems and a way of addressing the mother/son relationship that had been such an important part of his life (and work). Mrs Crane, like Mrs Williams, had been an overbearing mother whose neurotic affection had the effect of driving her son away from her. In this work the poet and his mother address each other in the afterlife. The lighting is gentle and, together with sound effects and the projection of abstract images and colours, represents the sea. This reflects the watery death and ocean floor resting place of the poet, both of which he refers to directly in the course of the performance. It is also a symbol of infinity. Grace Crane, like her son, has died, and her death somehow gives her this one final chance to communicate with him.

She reminds Hart of her remarkable dedication to his posthumous reputation while missing the irony that it was she who was partly responsible for the misery that led to his suicide, aged 32. As such, the piece, though apparently focused on a mother's continued love for and championing of her son, fits in with the rest of the Tennessee Williams oeuvre as a condemnation of the poisonous effect of many family relationships and as evidence of the vicissitudes of growing up gay in America.

The same year as *Steps Must Be Gentle*, *Clothes for a Summer Hotel* premiered at the Cort Theatre in New York – the last new, full-length play by Williams that would open on Broadway. Its failure was all the more disappointing given the inherently glamorous central characters, Zelda and F. Scott Fitzgerald, and the themes that the play explored. Tennessee subtitled the piece 'A Ghost Play' and populated the stage, alongside the Fitzgeralds, with other notable figures, including the macho novelist Ernest Hemingway and the wittily acerbic grande dame of the early twentieth-century English stage, Mrs Patrick Campbell. She was the sort of actress, talented but traumatic to work with (like Tallulah Bankhead and Bette Davis), with whom Tennessee had occasionally clashed during his career. In her later life she became, as people sometimes do, a caricature of herself – her own worst enemy. Despite this, Mrs Patrick Campbell inspired great affection, leading other theatre people to try to help her – help she sabotaged time and again, leading to the devastatingly accurate quip that she was like a sinking battleship, firing with all guns on any vessels sent to rescue her.

The critics chose to take the subtitle and the play itself at face value: a drama set in the grounds of the psychiatric hospital to which Zelda had been confined and in which she perished in a fire, featuring ghosts of celebrities and a number of, in effect, dream sequences. What, they wondered, was the point of it all? Was the playwright cannibalizing past artists in order to get some easily bought attention for his new drama? And was it not laziness to introduce yet another Rose-like character, in the person of Zelda Fitzgerald, driven mad by life? Following their cue from the professionals, the public stayed away and the show had a short run. This was another nail in the coffin of the writer's reputation and his already fragile self-esteem, but the pity of it is that he was justified, once again, in thinking that its failure was entirely undeserved. In fact not only was it a good play, it was one of the best of his later works – far more accessible and engaging than *Camino Real*, his much earlier dreamlike drama populated by literary characters.

Clothes for a Summer Hotel was clearer, easier to follow and, because it was essentially about the personal rather than the political, far more effective than *Camino Real*. Here he was indeed using well-known characters from the past, because they perfectly fitted the themes he wanted to discuss: the primacy of work to an artist; the necessary selfishness this involved; the struggles so many writers had/have with drink; and, one of his major pre-occupations – as strong here as in his masterpieces of the 1940s and 1950s – the tragedy of Time with its destruction of beauty.

As such, the play, despite being an admittedly minor one, deserves attention. Even before it begins, the stage directions that precede the first line are telling: F. Scott Fitzgerald is described as 'a man with blurred edges, a tentative manner, but with a surviving dignity and capacity for deep feeling'. In all of Williams's plays, dignity in survival was among the highest possible achievements a human could attain and here, as he approached his seventies with his body, mind and talent battered by a remorselessly self-destructive intake of alcohol and drugs, it was the most important clue that the playwright could offer to Fitzgerald's innate worth. Although Scott and Zelda clash throughout the play, and though the writer's sympathies are, inevitably, for damaged, mad, beautiful and doomed Zelda, she is not, as some thought, specifically another version of Rose. Though there are, as ever, echoes of the writer's sister, Zelda here is a real-life tragic female figure who went mad and was burned to death (seven years after her husband's alcoholism killed him) in the asylum in which she lived.

Zelda was an author and talent in her own right, and the clash between her talent and her husband's is crucial to the play. Both husband and wife, as doomed artists who live for their work, represent aspects of the playwright. Instead of cannibalizing people from his own life in order to create art (although the play does have some autobiographical elements), on this occasion he used historical figures. And why not? Dramatists from Aeschylus to Caryl Churchill via Shakespeare and Terence Rattigan have done the same. Using the famous to make his point, far from being lazy, was a way of universalizing the ideas he wanted to raise. But as he could do almost no right in the eyes of the critical establishment, this attempt to offer a fresh platform, drawn from the wider world and with a back story that was already known and could therefore let the playwright cut to the chase, was dismissed out of hand.

Clothes for a Summer Hotel begins with F. Scott Fitzgerald having travelled across America from Hollywood, where he is working on a film script, to visit his mentally ill wife, Zelda. He has been told she is much recovered, so is upset to find she is still far from well and has delusions about becoming a ballet dancer for the great Russian impresario Diaghilev. The play blends music and dance with the action in a way that was something of a signature for Tennessee, and does so in an attractive and atmospheric way. One of the scenes involves a party – a reference to the parties that punctuated Scott and Zelda's married life and which Scott was to satirize so well in *The Great Gatsby*. Far from being pleased to see her husband, Zelda burns with rage at the way she was expected, as a young woman, to subordinate herself wholly to his success, dimming her own talent at Scott's insistence lest it threaten to overshadow his own. The play moves back and forth in time. Zelda, as part of her war against her husband, recreates her affair with a dashing young French aviator.

The fluidity of time is used as a way of emphasizing its importance: the influence of the past and how ghosts from it continue to haunt us. This is typical Williams. Zelda mocks Scott

F. Scott Fitzgerald
and his wife Zelda,
central characters in
Tennessee's *Clothes for
a Summer Hotel.*

when he arrives at the asylum for the way the years have ravaged his
looks and added inches to his waistline, while even a mutual friend,
Gerald Murphy, cannot help pointing out, 'You were a remarkably
handsome young man, but – time has a habit of passing.' Another
theme is a reference to birds, with the creatures being associated
(as in *The Roman Spring of Mrs Stone*) with women. When one of
the asylum staff suggests Zelda behave delicately, she ripostes,
'Delicacy is not in the style of a hawk.' Arguing later with Scott,
she says, 'I have the eyes of a hawk, which is a bird of a nature as
predatory as a husband who appropriates your life as material for

his writing.' A case of the writer airing not just the historical Zelda's resentment at her husband but, perhaps, his own sense of guilt about having built a career from his dysfunctional family. As if responding to this, and to other people's accusations, he has Ernest Hemingway, in a row with Fitzgerald, insist that: 'You know as well as I do that every goddam character an honest writer creates is part of himself. Don't you? Well, *don't* you?'

Though his family provided Williams with his initial – and continuing – material, it had been his love of writing, his dedication to it and the sheer amount of work he put in that enabled his career to take off, and this is something that is central to the play. Fitzgerald at one point cries out: 'Writing calls for discipline! Continual!'; while Zelda says, 'Work – Loveliest of all four-letter words.' In *Clothes for a Summer Hotel*, Williams states, via Hemingway, the basic creed for all those who dedicate their lives to writing: 'Look, Scott, it's my profession to observe and interpret all kinds of human relations. That's how serious writers hire out to do. Maybe it's rough, this commitment, but we honour it with truth as we observe and interpret it.' Williams's interpretation was often couched in the poetic language for which he rightly became famous, and this play has its own examples of poetry, as when Zelda is in bed with her dashing French lover:

> Tonight . . . I thought I was holding your body against me inseparably close, so tight that I felt the blades of your bones carved to mine. You were bronze gold, you smelled of the sand and the sun (on a bed cooled by a Mediterranean Moon).

Creating poetry, creating plays, despite the succession of failures he had with them, was still, in 1980, central to his life. One of his poems referred to those, like him, who decide, despite being out of place as well as out of sorts, to plough on:

Those who ignore the appropriate time of their going
are the most valiant explorers,
going into a country that no one is meant to go into,
the time coming after that isn't meant to come after.
In the winter of cities.

His poems are even more personal than his plays, perhaps
because, as an art form, poetry lends itself better to sadness than
to joy. In 'Life Story', which has a typically dark humour at the very
end, he describes the choreography and script involved in the sort
of casual pick-ups he had had since he first found his sexual stride.
It is a short poem and deserves to be quoted in full:

After you've been to bed together for the first time,
without the advantage or disadvantage of any prior
acquaintance,
the other party very often says to you,
Tell me about yourself, I want to know all about you,
what's your story? And you think maybe they really and truly do

sincerely want to know your life story, and so you light up
a cigarette and begin to tell it to them, the two of you
lying together in completely relaxed positions
like a pair of rag dolls a bored child dropped on a bed.

You tell them your story, or as much of your story
as time or a fair degree of prudence allows, and they say,
Oh, oh, oh, oh, oh,
each time a little more faintly, until the oh
is just an audible breath, and then of course

there's some interruption. Slow room service comes up
with a bowl of melting ice cubes, or one of you rises to pee

and gaze at himself with mild astonishment in the bathroom mirror.
And then, the first thing you know, before you've had time
to pick up where you left off with your enthralling life story,
they're telling you their life story, exactly as they'd intended to all along,

and you're saying, Oh, oh, oh, oh, oh,
each time a little more faintly, the vowel at last becoming
no more than an audible sigh,
as the elevator, halfway down the corridor and a turn to the left,
draws one last, long, deep breath of exhaustion
and stops breathing forever. Then?

Well, one of you falls asleep
and the other one does likewise with a lighted cigarette in his mouth,
and that's how people burn to death in hotel rooms.

The hotel rooms in which he found temporary comfort were
in Europe as much as America, and though his long-term lovers,
Pancho Rodriguez y Gonzalez and Frank Merlo, had been darkly
good-looking, he had since developed a taste for blond Italians,
an interest described in his poem 'The Blond Mediterraneans':

It is the blond Mediterraneans you know the ones with Norman blood in them
under thirty unmarried given a fine bone structure on which they've
accrued
not a pound of excess weight
I mean the ones who solicit with such discretion and grace
on the Cuorso

or lean with so natural a provocation on the bone-white
balustrade
of the main square . . .

In the poem he describes finding just such a man, but the
beautiful blond's eye is on the main chance and, more specifically,
the biggest available wallet:

I never saw him again. I understand that he was overwhelmed by
the
charms of
some enormously wealthy munitions king from Hamburg . . .

With this sort of experience, it is hardly surprising that Williams
found work so much more satisfying, ultimately, than the sex he
relentlessly pursued. In *Clothes for a Summer Hotel*, he argues that
creativity is what gives meaning to *any* writer's life. Words are not
just a raison d'être. They are a legacy, the equivalent of children,
the passing on of genes. As Zelda says, 'Words are the love acts of
writers.' Without writing, without words, life is not just pointless,
it is unendurable. This time it is Hemingway, talking of his suicide,
who speaks for Tennessee: 'I chose to blast my brains out for
no reason but the good and sufficient reason that my work was
finished, strong, hard work all done – no reason for me to continue.'
In a way, this foreshadowed Williams's own death, which was a form
of suicide by substance abuse, made tragic by the fact that he still
felt he had things to say and creative ways of saying them. He had,
on several occasions, told friends and acquaintances he would like,
when the time came, to be buried at sea, like his poetic hero Hart
Crane, and he justified this, too, through one of the characters in the
play: Zelda says, of the ashes that she would be reduced to when she
died in the asylum fire, 'Persuade them somehow to scatter all to the
wind to be blown out to sea: that's the purification, *give me that*!'

Though *Clothes for a Summer Hotel* is not one of Williams's greatest works, it has poetry, drama and humour, the latter being a regular feature of his writing that is often overlooked. It proves that his ability to dramatize the human condition, the need for love and the power of words, the excitement of sex and the pitilessness of time, were still there. This blend of the fiery and the delicate may not have reached the heights of *A Streetcar Named Desire* or *The Glass Menagerie,* but it offered theatregoers exactly what they had always responded to in his work. However, when presented with it in a new play, audiences unaccountably rejected it as tired, third-rate or toothless. The play closed after just fifteen performances.

The contrast between this latest slap in the face and the official esteem in which his past body of work was held, was emphasized by his having been awarded, that same year, the Presidential Medal of Freedom by President Carter. Such awards tend to be a gesture from the powers that be, but on this occasion there may have been a more personal reason for giving it: Jimmy Carter, whose own luck was very much down at that point (he was to lose the 1980 election to the Governor of California, Ronald Reagan), was himself a keen – and quite good – writer of poetry in his spare time. He is currently the only ex-President of the United States to have published a volume of poetry (*Always a Reckoning*).

That Tennessee still had dramatic teeth was shown in his next play, but, ironically, he turned them on himself. In August 1981 his highly autobiographical *Something Cloudy, Something Clear* opened at the Bouwerie Lane Theatre, New York, performed by the Jean Cocteau Repertory company and directed by Eve Adamson, who would later write a brief but perceptive introduction to the published version of the play. The title refers to the eyes of the central character, August – an appropriate name, considering the piece's summer setting. August, like Tennessee himself as a young man, has one eye clear and one that, due to a cataract, is cloudy. This is no coincidence: August *is* Tennessee. He is so doubly because we see him both as he was in 1940 (when his cataract was noticeable and in need of medical attention) and as he is forty years later. The play is highly and unashamedly autobiographical: it deals with his struggles as a young artist in a way that presages his later sense of selling out artistically for the sake of financial expediency and fame. At its heart is the affair he had on the beaches of Provincetown with Kip Kiernan in the summer of 1940. Rather as he did in *Clothes for a Summer Hotel*, he blurs the line between the past and present, but it is done more directly and effectively here. August does not so much switch between past and present as inhabit both simultaneously. Similarly, the other main character, Clare, is also in the present but aware of her future and therefore looking back at herself even as she lives her life going forwards.

Something Cloudy, Something Clear exposes the tribulations of a playwright's existence – the need for major rewrites, the rapacious-ness of producers, the dependence, for a play's success, on the presence of a star (usually female) and the need for that performer to shine on the night. More specifically, it recreates Tennessee's first gay relationship, but it also refers forwards to his most important (and, eventually, equally doomed) one, with Frank Merlo, who makes a brief appearance. This is more than just a history. The author takes real people and events but applies his craft to make the story work dramatically, in the imaginatively modern way that was coming to typify his work, but which failed to bring back the audiences who still attended revivals of his earlier plays. In her introduction to *Something Cloudy, Something Clear*, Eve Adamson describes the critics as being unjustifiably unkind, suggesting their attitude was as absurd as it would have been for art critics to attack Picasso for moving on from his Blue Period.

This being a play rather than a history, Williams created an imaginary character, Clare, who at first appears to be Kip's sister but later, in a series of revelations, turns out to be more attached and less related to him than that, as well as having a far darker past than she first lets on. This past violently catches up with her on the beach where August is spending the summer in a run-down but picturesque shack. Violence is one of the undercurrents of the play; another is illness. Williams had been the victim of violence himself as a young man, beaten up by 'tricks' he had sex with, while more recently he had been mugged. As well as physical force, he addresses the more insidious form of violence represented by one person effectively forcing himself on another.

Here it is the young August who, desperately in love with the beautiful Kip, doesn't so much seduce him as demand sex in return for the promise of financial support when they move back to New York. What August is offering is protection from a hostile world, rather in the way that, throughout history, older men have offered protection to nubile young women. The play makes clear, from Kip's sullen response the morning after he reluctantly sleeps with August, that the protection is more akin to the physically violent 'protection' offered by mobsters. That Clare's past arrives in the shape of a mobster makes the parallels very clear.

Given that in real life Tennessee and Kip's relationship was happy (even if Tennessee was the keener when it came to sex and Kip left him for a woman) it is extraordinary that he should write a play where he presents himself, in the form of August, in an unattractive, even predatory, light. The play is remarkable especially as it is about someone Williams felt huge affection for at the time and a romantic sense of loss about ever after. It had been, he often told friends, the purest of his many affairs. Yet in *Something Cloudy, Something Clear*, the fictionalized Kip is only really attracted to or interested in Clare (who didn't exist in real life but onstage represents young women in general) and regards August as just another gay who lusts after him. So in this play he is not doing what many writers would – casting a golden nostalgic glow over a youthful seaside summer romance. On the contrary, he is expressing a sort of disgust at sexual desire, presenting it as something sordid and closely linked to power – not

The Finborough Theatre production (directed by Tamara Harvey) of *Something Cloudy, Something Clear*, 2003. James Hillier as August, Bruce Godfree as Kip and Juliet Rylance as Clare.

just an exchange of bodily fluids but an expression of one human's dominance over another, as expressed by penetrative sex. At one point, Clare accuses August of 'violating' Kip's body. Later, when negotiating terms for the three of them possibly staying together in New York, she makes it clear that a cuddle and even a caress might be tolerated. What is clearly not to be allowed is anal sex. Elsewhere in the play August pays a drunken sailor to allow August to bugger him. What Williams does here is to place his physical relations with Kip, despite his professed love for the boy, on fundamentally the same basis as that with the sailor – an animal act that only one of them enjoys. Far from being an expression of love, sex in this instance is entirely selfish. Williams is casting himself not as Blanche DuBois, but as Stanley Kowalski.

All this suggests that in this play Williams was not just drawing on people and actions from his past, as he so often did; he was distilling the self-hatred and regret that had always dogged his relationship with sex. He was flogging himself onstage for the faults he had always been aware of but unable to overcome. His long experience of paying for sex, whether casually or, on occasion, for longer-term engagements, is mercilessly exposed. There is nothing here of a jaded sophisticate shrugging off a lifetime's use of young hustlers. It's more a case of an elderly penitent looking back in shame. The most painful way of punishing himself is not to try to differentiate between an unsullied first love and the animal lust for a succession of rent boys and pick-ups. He punishes himself in the most painful way possible – by degrading that first love, making himself appear no better with Kip than the dirty old men who had also made advances on him that summer.

For a playwright who was known to place his life on the stage, this was an amazingly brave, if self-destructive (as ever), thing to do. He gives August a line that summed up his own subconscious attitude to relationships, an attitude that inevitably sank them all: 'Being loved is a hard thing to believe.' He could never quite accept that anyone could love him, so he acted as if the love was doomed, which became a self-fulfilling prophecy. Noël Coward dealt with the same problem in his poem 'I am No Good at Love'. Among other autobiographical features referenced in the play is the way, when attracted to someone in his youth, Williams would tremble with nerves: 'I – when I want something very badly, I . . . start shaking all over.' As a young man he had the additional affliction of blushing deep red if someone he fancied looked him directly in the eye. A further and more fundamental reference to his life comes in a line that distils the essence of much of his entire literary output: 'Aren't families awful people?' Naturally, he also talks about a writer's work, and his own versatility: 'I write plays. Stories. Poems.' He acknowledges what people have always said about his work – how it draws on a limited number of themes – but defends this: 'Artists always continue a theme with variations. If lucky, several themes with numerous variations.'

One of these recurrent themes is madness. Kip isn't mad as such, but we learn he has a brain tumour that will kill him, and it affects not just his balance but also his ability to concentrate. It is no coincidence, knowing Tennessee's obsession with mental illness, that both August and Clare compare Kip, a beautiful dancer, to Nijinsky, the genius whose early onset of insanity is as much a part of his enduring legend as his skill as a dancer. Williams would bring Nijinsky into another play, *A Cavalier for Milady*, as a character onstage. The writer's fear of illness, allied to a conviction that he was destined to an early death, is also given full rein in *Something Cloudy, Something Clear*, as not only is Kip dying from his brain tumour, but Clare has a fatal illness too, and neither is expected to survive long after the end of summer. The real-life Kip had about four years left after his seaside romance with Tennessee ended, but for dramatic purposes the playwright makes Kip's demise imminent.

Williams's talent enabled him to immortalize Kip, preserving his name and beauty for posterity. He left a less attractive epitaph for himself, and his profession, in a speech by the cynical and manipulative theatre producer Maurice Fiddler, who dismisses all playwrights as failures waiting to happen:

> Playwrights are spawned in tenements and bordellos, then they graduate to the YMCA, then they graduate suddenly to Park Avenue apartments and grand hotels, and then they lose everything but their taste for booze and their outraged, outrageous egos, and finally, usually, they die in Bowery gutters from delirium tremens or an overdose of narcotics.

The speech was an eerily accurate prophecy of the death that its author endured less than two years after it was first heard. In his case, he died not in a slum but in a good hotel, though his death, as if to make sure, was from not one but both the potential causes Maurice Fiddler sneered at.

Another of his early 1980s plays, proof of Williams's continuing productivity despite all the odds, was *Will Mr Merriweather Return from Memphis?* This is a light, comic piece. Ghosts appear – not just memories but actual ghosts who are summoned by the two clairvoyants, Louise and Nora, who are near neighbours in Tiger Town, a fictional representation of St Louis. The Mr Merriweather of the title is Louise's ex-lodger, on whom she pinned her romantic hopes but who has gone to Memphis, much to Louise's distress. She berates her daughter, Gloria, for wearing skimpy dresses when she goes to the library, where the local youths wait for her, hoping for sex. Gloria's real affection is for Richard, a handsome young man whose shyness and stutter are cured when Gloria seduces him in the local park. Their lovemaking is watched over by three Old Crones – a composite of the Furies and Norns of ancient Greek and Norse mythology, respectively.

Back at the house, Louise and Nora summon a further apparition – this time of the poet Rimbaud, in the period after he had had a leg amputated. He is being cared for in his wheelchair by his sister, Isabelle. It is usually the younger Rimbaud, the precocious teenage poet, who interests writers and readers. Williams, drawn to failures and those whose youthful looks have vanished, characteristically portrays him in his later, post-poetic, ruined state, on the verge of death. The play ends on a bittersweet note: Mr Merriweather does indeed return from Memphis into Louise's arms, but when Nora's dead husband appears to her, it is to tell her he was always unfaithful to her. As he does so he plays the banjo, whose music we have heard in the distance at several points in the play.

Written and published (though not performed) that same, productive year, was another surreal work, the wonderfully titled *Now the Cats with Jewelled Claws*. Though it doesn't feature ghosts or dead writers, it does once more have the symbolic figure of Death – in the form of a hunched old man, carrying a sandwich board emblazoned with 'Mr Black'. Set in a restaurant that has a gay middle-aged manager and a pregnant waitress with a black eye, there are two couples who come in: a pair of elderly ladies, Bea and Madge, and two gay men, Young Man 1 and Young Man 2. Young Man 1 is desperately in love with Young Man 2 and wants to have a monogamous relationship with him. His lover, however, believes in having sex as often as possible with a variety of partners. He makes the point by arranging an assignation in the restaurant lavatory with the manager.

During the one-act play there is dancing, singing and poetry. The play ends dramatically when the Young Men, having left the restaurant, are involved in a traffic accident. Young Man 2 is killed. Young Man 1 is brought back into the restaurant, and the play ends with him, distraught, accepting comfort and consolation from the manager. Bizarre though it is, there is a beauty and poetry about *Now the Cats with Jewelled Claws* that is very engaging. The poem 'They that Come Late to the Dance' is sung by the manager as Bea and Madge dance. While an engaging image in itself, is also something of a late-life explanation of how those (like Tennessee Williams) who start their sex life later than most, can have an intense, almost frenzied, sex drive – just as converts to a religion are often more actively devoted to it than those brought up in the faith.

They that come late to the dance
more wildly must dance than the rest
though the strings of the violins
are a thousand knives in their breast.

They that come late to the dance
must dance till their slippers are thin
and the last white notes of the flute
are lost in the dawn-blowing wind.

They that come late to the dance
must dance till the lanterns expire
and the hearts they uncovered too late
are broken before they can tire.

Dance is seen as well as spoken about, as if Tennessee, still
pushing theatrical boundaries, wanted to blend dance, song and
drama together in something that was definitely not a musical but
was certainly not a conventional play. Time, 'the enemy of us all'
that had haunted him throughout his life, was now running out. Yet
even at this stage, he showed why his legendary status in American
theatre was deserved, in a final (in his lifetime) play which, though
rarely performed, is actually one of his best.

A House Not Meant to Stand was given three productions in three
versions, from 1980 to 1982, starting as a one-acter before being
developed into a full-length work all at the Goodman Theatre,
Chicago. The final one, published by New Directions in 2008 with
a fascinating introduction by Gregory Mosher, the theatre's artistic
director at the time, opened on 2 April 1982. Based on a one-act
play called Some Problems for the Moose Lodge, A House Not Meant to
Stand opens in a dilapidated Southern mansion, one that is barely
standing after years of neglect and which lets in water from the
violent storm that rages outside throughout the play. In his stage
directions at the beginning of the script, Tennessee describes the
play as 'my kind of Southern Gothic spook drama' and is clear that
'the dilapidation of this house is a metaphor for the state of society'.
This second assertion, allied to some overtly political statements
by Cornelius, the appalling patriarch of a profoundly dysfunctional

family, suggests the play is making a point about contemporary American society. While there *are* elements of this (Williams satirizes the increasingly prominent presence of the American Religious Right, in the heavily pregnant shape of Stacey, the fiancée of one of Cornelius's children), the play is a brilliant comedy with gifts of parts for actors of both sexes and all ages.

The usual autobiographical elements are here, and will be discussed in a moment, but what strikes the reader (it is more likely to be read than seen, sadly), is the sheer comic force. The Southern setting, the American speech patterns, the desperate attempts to keep madness, old-age and death at bay are all classic Tennessee Williams, but overall the black comedy and the boisterous, over-the-top pace bordering on farce and delight in exuberant sexuality constantly remind one of the English playwright, Joe Orton. Williams was a fan of Orton, whose comedies, including *Entertaining Mr Sloane*, *Loot* and *What the Butler Saw*, established him as London's most outrageous young playwright. Orton's premature end in 1967 – beaten to death with a hammer by his long-term lover, Kenneth Halliwell, who then committed suicide – was as grotesque as the situations he subjected his characters to onstage.

A House Not Meant to Stand, though Ortonesque – even down to a hidden stash of money, as in *Loot* – owes its force to Williams's back catalogue of characters and situations, allied to an entirely fresh plot of his own devising, in a play that perfectly combines very dark comedy with, simultaneously, something that is desperately sad. The way the sadness runs through the play, even while some of the things that arouse the audience's pity also produce laughter, means that the conclusion, with humour and heartache in tandem up to the very end, is somehow wholly in keeping with what has preceded it. There isn't so much a change of tone as a choice of ending on a melody that has been playing throughout, even if drowned at times by livelier rhythms and gaudier songs. As the play is relatively little known and as it shows that, even at the end of his life, Williams was a major talent, it is worth going into what happens in some detail.

The house referred to in the title is the family home of the husband and wife Cornelius and Bella McCorkle, who are in their late sixties or early seventies. The play opens with their return from Memphis and the funeral of one of their children (all of whom are young adults), a son called Chips. We learn that Chips was gay and an alcoholic. There are two other children: Charlie, unbeknown to his parents, has returned to the house, bringing with him his heavily pregnant fiancée, of whom they know nothing; the third child and only daughter, Joanie, is a highly sexed young woman who has been committed to a psychiatric ward. Cornelius, an aggressive homo-phobic thug with ambitions in local politics, wants to have Bella, an unhealthily overweight woman, committed to an asylum, too.

Bella's trump card, to Cornelius's fury, is that her side of the family, the Dacies, left a fortune in cash from bootlegging liquor sales. She is the only person who knows where this semi-legendary money is, and her refusal to reveal its whereabouts means Cornelius can't have her taken away as he would then lose his only chance of getting his hands on the cash he needs to fuel his ill-advised campaign for office. The couple's equally elderly neighbours are Emerson and Jessie Sykes. He is an oversexed, borderline senile businessman with shady finances. He hopes to establish a chain of cheap 'motels' that are, in effect, little more than bordellos. Jessie spends whatever cash she can get her hands on, on cosmetic surgery. She has the same inappropriately strong sex drive as her husband, except that the objects of her affection are young men, whom she is happy to spend money on in return for sexual favours.

The autobiographical elements here are obvious: Cornelius is named after Tennessee's father, while his ill-conceived political ambitions are a direct reference to those of his brother, Dakin, who spent a small fortune on various runs for office. Making fun of these onstage can't have helped the already strained relations between the two men. Bella's name, it has been suggested by commentators, may be an amalgamation of Cornelius Williams's two sisters, Isabella and Ella. Bella's name is often bellowed by Cornelius in the play, and it seems likely that it is an ironic reference to the way 'Stella!' is famously bellowed by a distraught Stanley Kowalski in *A Streetcar Named Desire*. (This iconic moment in *Streetcar* was satirized in an episode of the American sitcom *Modern Family* and also in the darkly comic cartoon series *Family Guy*.) Dacie, Bella's maiden name, is not a million miles from Dakin, the name of Edwina Williams's family, while even more directly, McCorkle was the maiden name of one of Tennessee's grandmothers.

Fraught though his later years were, he retained a capacity for friendship and for a defiant *joie de vivre*. Tennessee laughing with British actress Charlotte Rampling at Cannes film festival in 1976.

Cornelius and Edwina, like the play's Cornelius and Bella, had two sons and one girl. In both families one boy was gay, one straight and the girl went mad and was incarcerated. Cornelius's dismissal of Tennessee as 'Miss Nancy' is mirrored in the relentlessly homophobic way the Cornelius of the play rubbishes the memory of his recently deceased son, Chips: 'I remember when he was voted prettiest girl at Pascagoula High.' We never see Joanie, just hear about her in a desperate letter sent by her to Bella. Joanie's misfortunes and rackety life incite laughter instead of pity, rather as happens with another unfortunate child in Simon Gray's *Quartermaine's Terms*, where laconic accounts of disasters that befall her are increasingly hilarious, despite the distress they represent. Bella's reaction to Joanie's predicament – even though she shares the same risk, from Cornelius, of incarceration – demonstrates the bizarre disconnect that she has from her children's lives. She is more concerned about Joanie's use of the F-word than her being in a mental home or having been conducting an affair with a married man.

Bella, fat, out of breath, disconnected and not very bright, could be a stock comic character, but in Tennessee's hands she is something of a martyred earth-mother, a woman who for all her inadequacies is driven by love for her children – specifically, for a fondly remembered past when they *were* children. Charlie, her surviving son, may be a wastrel with a massive sex drive, but he comes across as a fundamentally decent man, happy to marry his very pregnant lover, defensive of his dead brother's memory and loyally standing up for his mother against his father. However hopeless she seems now, Bella must have had some maternal abilities, if only an inherent kindness, to have produced such an affectionate and loyal son.

While the rest of the characters create a whirlwind of avarice, lust and betrayal that matches the extraordinary storm outside, Bella is determined to pass on the Dacie money to her surviving children and her soon-to-be-born grandchild. She is also, during the evening, trying to recreate a happier past by conjuring the ghosts of her children, by arranging the kitchen the way it was when they were little. As part of this plan she gets Charlie to bring back into the kitchen the childhood chairs that Cornelius has long since banished to an outhouse. At the end of the play, despite what threatens to be the last-minute theft of the Dacie cash by the rapacious Mrs Sykes, the money is safely handed over to those she loves, via the dignified young local doctor, an amalgam of Dr John in *Summer and Smoke* and the young doctor in *Suddenly Last Summer*. Bella has been told where to find the money by the ghost of her recently dead son, while at the end, the ghosts of all of her three children, as children, come into the kitchen, where she asks them, in a scene that mirrors the family meal in *The Glass Menagerie*, to say grace.

Here, specifically, Williams is not simply repeating a scene in his first big hit. He is embodying the echoes of early family life that ran through so much of his work, looking back to a time that he could never quite come to terms with, however often he addressed the subject in his plays and however genuine his sympathy for his father as a man, after Cornelius had died. There, as Shakespeare would have put it, was the rub. For as the spotlight of his resentment and anger dimmed on Cornelius, so it had sharpened and brightened against Edwina, the mother he came to blame for the emotional wasteland of the parent–child relationship in the Williams household. Bella's coarse, gauche persona (everything Edwina would have looked down on) is the unlikely vessel for the writer's long-delayed wish fulfilment: a mother who loves her children and lavishes uncomplicated affection on them. Among the ghosts of the children who answer her summons to the family table is, surely, that of the young Tennessee Williams.

Moving as this is, the overriding emotion of the evening is laughter. As mentioned, Cornelius does make one or two brief political speeches, addressed directly to the audience (as several speeches are, by different characters), but these should not be taken as the playwright making political points via his play. They are set up to be undercut by humour, to be terminated by a laugh, as in the following:

> CORNELIUS: Sinister these times. – East – West – armed to the teeth. – Nukes and neutrons. – Invested so much in every type of munitions, yes, even in germs, cain't afford not to use them, fight it out to the death of every human inhabitant of the earth if not the planet's destruction – opposed by no one . . .

> EMERSON [*indifferently*]: No shit.

A House Not Meant to Stand made it to a festival in Miami for a month, where it was described by one reviewer as 'The best thing Williams has written since *Small Craft Warnings*', but it failed to transfer to New York, not least because its author's reputation for commercial failure meant that raising money for the inevitably expensive hire of a New York theatre (however small) and the necessary publicity budget and other associated costs was simply too much of a risk for producers to take at this stage.

The result, for this comedy, was tragic. Had it gone to New York and been given the praise it deserves, Tennessee Williams's theatre career could have ended on an unexpected high – the happy ending that the American Dream always promises. Instead, it was staged in Chicago, the town where his first great success, *The Glass Menagerie*, was launched. Though there is sadness in his rejection by New York, there is something satisfyingly apt in his career as a major twentieth-century playwright beginning and ending in the same city. It is equally, if less happily, fitting that New York, the city where his early triumphs were replaced with critical and commercial destruction, should be where he met his death. In the ten months between the final Chicago opening of *A House Not Meant to Stand* and his own curtain call he had, as always, spent a lot of time travelling. He visited London, where he was now more appreciated than in Manhattan, and he also returned to his beloved Italy, visiting Sicily and Rome. Back in the States, the academic establishment was determined to recognize his past contribution to American literature while he was still alive. In August, Harvard awarded him an honorary degree.

On Christmas Eve 1982 friends had to break into his house in Key West, after he hadn't been seen or heard from for days. He was found, collapsed, surrounded by pills. After coming out of hospital he paid a last visit to his home and gave his housekeeper a much larger than usual cheque. That, and the uncharacteristic kiss he gave her as he said goodbye and headed for New York, was an unspoken farewell to the house that had been one of the few fixed points in a life of hotels and rented apartments. In *The Night of the Iguana* he had referred to the unbearable pain in the eyes of Hart Crane. Those around him, from friends to employees to acquaintances, saw something similar in the months before and after he left Key West for the last time. He may not consciously have wanted his life to end, given he had survived so much and for so long, but, on the other hand, a line from *Camino Real* seems sadly apt: 'There is a time for departure, even where there is no certain place to go.'

February 1983 saw him, after what proved to be a final trip to Sicily, at Manhattan's Hotel Elysée, where he stayed in the suitably named Sunset Suite. Equally appropriate was the name of the hotel itself, with its connotations of Europe (as in the Elysée Palace, official home of the President of France) and of the classical myths from the Mediterranean world he had loved all his life – the Elysian Fields, where the souls of heroes spent eternity. In view of his propensity to put the dead in his later plays, the name seemed particularly appropriate. It also lent itself to his characteristically sexual sense of humour – he referred to it as the 'Easy Lay'. It was here, sometime on the night of 24 or early morning of 25 February, that he died. His travelling companion and helper, John Ueker, apparently heard

Tennessee Williams commemorated on the St Louis Walk of Fame, in the city he longed to leave but in which, ironically, he is buried.

nothing amiss – and in any case had standing instructions not to disturb him. Besides, even if there had been the sound of a collapse, Tennessee had a long history of slumping to the floor, with a bump, in a stupefied state. A variation on this affinity with the carpet was a party trick of his, when bored or nervous, to pretend to have a heart attack and die. Once safely carried out of the room he wished to leave, he would spring (if that's quite the word for someone so podgy, ill and arthritic) back to life. When found on the morning of 25 February, though, all life had gone, for ever. His exit, this final time, had been for real.

It was reported that he had died, accidentally, by choking on the cap of a bottle of pills. Death by choking was one of his great fears, so if that had been the manner of his passing, it would have been particularly unpleasant for him. It was certainly a plausible explanation, as he had a habit of placing pills into the bottle lid and then – rather gracefully, as if pouring a miniature cup of tea – tipping them into his mouth. Whether this was the actual cause became a matter of dispute, not least because, with the death of anyone so famous, conspiracy theories kick in soon after the event is reported. Dakin, his brother, certainly suspected foul play, while it has been variously suggested that the bottle cap was an invention or that it was present, but in his mouth, not blocking his airway. Whatever the exact manner of his passing, it was taking so many pills, washed down with alcohol, in the course of his life that killed him. The only real surprise about his death was that it was such a long time coming. His youthful notebooks record a constant succession of stomach and bowel complaints, while his liver and kidneys coped, in the course of his adult life, with far more punishment than those of most men (especially of his size) could have endured.

But then endurance against the odds and despite all predictions was what Tennessee Williams specialized in. His female characters, even the doomed ones, are, on their own terms, survivors until the final, irreversible collapse. And even then they face catastrophe – as Blanche faced the walk to the asylum – not just with dignity but with a real sense of grace. To have made it to his early seventies was an extraordinary achievement, as remarkable as his ability to keep producing work in experimental styles and of the remarkable quality of, for example, *Something Cloudy, Something Clear*.

He had often expressed the wish to be buried at sea, just like (and ideally near the same spot as) Hart Crane. By a curious oversight, however, this was not specified in his will, leaving Dakin Williams as the next of kin free to decide against this, on the rather macabre grounds that a literary figure as important as his brother should be buried in a grave that could be visited by his fans. Worse than this, Dakin insisted on interring him next to their mother, whom Tennessee had come to look back on with hatred, in the family plot in St Louis – the industrial city where he had been profoundly unhappy and from which he couldn't wait to escape. He had been able to do so in life, thanks to his talent, but, though his plays would continue to let his spirit speak to generations of theatregoers, his body, instead of being placed to rest in the fluidity, grace and poetry of the ocean, was placed where he would have least wanted, caged like so many of the wild of heart with whom he had populated his plays.

7

Afterlife: Into the Twenty-first Century

Dakin was correct that the world would continue to be fascinated by his brother, but this took the form not of graveside tourism, but of continued revivals of his plays. More recently, there has been increasing attention paid not just to the work Tennessee created at his prime, but to the very plays that drew so much critical flack: the many apparent failures of the last twenty years of his life. There have also been discoveries of unpublished and unperformed work. This has been brought to life on the stage in the early years of the twenty-first century, in a secular resurrection that has seen Tennessee Williams rise in flame like a phoenix. That resurrection was not helped by his friend Maria Britneva, Lady St Just, in the years between his death and her own in 1994, when she allocated herself the role of literary executor – the person who guards the reputation of the deceased writer by authorizing, or not, productions of his plays and deciding what could or could not be quoted, published (whether play, story, journal or letters) or performed.

A controversial figure in her own lifetime, the knives have been out for her since she died – twenty years of bitterness at her high-handed control of the Williams estate bubbling over in print. That there has been an explosion of material from, and writing about, Tennessee Williams, suggests that the criticism is valid, not least the assertion that she awarded herself far more authority in such dealings than she had been actually empowered with in his will. This had left her a trustee of his finances, which had been arranged so that after

Tennessee and Maria Britneva, Lady St Just, in 1950. Maria longed to be his wife and, after his death, controversially took control of his literary estate. She also published a book of their correspondence.

his death, his royalties would continue to provide Rose with a home and comforts. Touchingly, the terms of the trust specifically say that the trustees' duty is not just to provide for her needs but for her pleasures – for the little treats and kindnesses she so enjoyed. Maria immediately expanded her remit to include the role of literary executor. She stamped on Lyle Leverich's proposed biography, even though Tennessee had asked him to write it. It was not until the year after her death that Leverich was able to publish it, taking Williams's life and career up to the opening of *The Glass Menagerie*. After Leverich's own death, the baton was taken up by John Lahr, a distinguished theatre historian. His biography of Williams, already mentioned in this book, was widely praised when it was published in 2014.

Maria Britneva came to be in this controversial position because she was an old friend of the playwright's. Born in 1921 in Russia (though she, like him, was to knock a few years off her age in due course), she was a petite, dynamic, driven individual. She claimed to be a White Russian from a grand family, but much of the background story she presented after fleeing to England was fictional – or at least wildly exaggerated. Her future mother-in-law, the Dowager Lady St Just, was to dismiss her as 'that little Bolshevik'. Maria met Tennessee in 1948 in England through John Gielgud, who was directing the first London production of *The Glass Menagerie*. She had studied ballet and begun a career onstage before an injury led her to change direction and become an actress. She had some talent and eventually played Blanche in a production of *A Streetcar Named Desire*. The result was not entirely satisfactory and, though Tennessee told her to her face that she was wonderful in the role, to a friend he said that until he had seen Maria in the part he had not realized how bad a play it was!

Maria claimed that Tennessee based the character of Maggie in *A Cat on a Hot Tin Roof* on her, and given the way she fought for life and was happy to claw any female rival for his affections (not least Tallulah Bankhead), she may have been right. In 1956 she married Peter Grenfell, Lord St Just, thus acquiring a title. She bore him two daughters and was by all accounts a devoted mother, though she seems to have been a semi-detached wife. This was made easier by her husband's frequent absences in search of other sexual partners and his occasional spells in psychiatric hospitals. The presence of mental illness in her life gave her and Tennessee something in common beyond their shared love of theatre. A huge fan of his work, she was determined to be part of his inner circle and saw herself as the wife he might (and in her eyes, despite all the evidence to the contrary should) have had. Vivacious and a great gossip, she had a marked ability to cheer him up, and he was happy to indulge this, though by the end of his life he seemed to have tired of her. Dakin believed, to his dying day, that Tennessee was going to write Maria out of his will and that she was somehow behind his untimely death. That idea is worth a play in itself.

Lady St Just was barely mentioned in his *Memoirs* of 1975, which confirmed to those hostile to her that she was far less important a part of the writer's life than she liked to claim. Typical of her, she rectified this after his death when, in 1990, she published *Five O'Clock Angel*, a book of their correspondence. This was meant as a riposte to her enemies and to stake her claim on his friendship for posterity. The fact that almost all the letters were from him to her, as he didn't keep hers to him, rather undermined her central thesis. After death loosened her grip, the job of bringing Tennessee Williams into the twenty-first century was able to begin in earnest, and his star has risen again in the years that have followed.

It is the autobiographical nature of his works that is a large part of the attraction. Yet there is more to them than this. What they represent (albeit to differing degrees) is a demonstration of the continued fertility of his imagination. His later work was very much of and occasionally ahead of its time – part of the new wave of theatre in the late 1960s and beyond. This was a movement he understood and admired; he was a particular fan of Harold Pinter, though he understandably felt threatened by some of the other young playwrights who emerged at this time, specifically Edward Albee, author of the coruscating drama *Who's Afraid of Virginia Woolf?*

Modern directors, producers and audiences have realized that the theatre critics who accused Williams of mining old seams with increasingly feeble returns were missing the point. Yes, he was often dealing with the same issues, springing as they did from his own experience, but they have a universal application and appeal. His later plays presented the themes in fresh, imaginative ways and different styles. As with any experiment, sometimes this worked and sometimes it didn't. The backwards looks, however, were not the playwright's, but the critics'. Having berated him for writing plays about the same themes, they equally attacked him for not having written in the same old style. Given this situation, he could never win, and the realization ate away at his confidence and artistic self-esteem. His determination to carry on writing despite this is all the more heroic.

His later plays often had small casts and were designed to be performed in small spaces, so it is natural that recent productions of them have been off-Broadway or off-West End. The tiny but terrific Finborough Theatre in London's Earl's Court, for example, staged *Something Cloudy, Something Clear*, in a production directed by Tamara Harvey, recreating the Provincetown beach on a stage smaller than many people's living rooms. The intimacy that this created was part of the production's success. Another small London theatre that had a notable success this way was the King's Head, Islington, an iconic pub theatre in north London, founded in the early 1970s by Dan Crawford, an American expat who turned the pub's back room into one of London's most extraordinary theatre spaces. The room had, for a time, been used for boxing matches, so this was a case where the phrase 'punching above your weight' was fully justified in relation to the little theatre's big achievements. The King's Head's revival of *Vieux Carré*, directed by Robert Chevara, was a revelation. Far from being substandard later work, this proved to be a fascinating piece packed with typical Tennessee Williams characters – not a pastiche but a distillation. It was a summary, or a snapshot, then, and not the caricature some critics made it out to be when it was first performed in 1977.

But then London has always had an affinity with Tennessee Williams – as well as with Arthur Miller and Edward Albee. Miller, in his last years, preferred to have his work staged in London, finding West End audiences more appreciative than their Broadway counterparts. But though British audiences enjoy many American writers – with Eugene O'Neill another favourite – they have a special affection for Tennessee. It would be untrue to say that this was, at first, a mutual attraction. He had taken against John Gielgud, one of the greatest men of twentieth-century English theatre, when Gielgud directed *The Glass Menagerie*. In his journal, Tennessee wrote, 'An air of hopelessness on this island, the people grim, cold, unpleasant. The upper society quite heartless. Snobs and hypocrites to a shocking degree.' To be fair, he wasn't in the best of moods when he wrote that, as his latest sexual partner had just left: 'One rather delectable red-head served me occasionally but had now gone to sea.' England, still shattered by the Second World War, was bomb-damaged and enduring worse rationing than at the height of the conflict. Food in London, other than at a handful of expensive restaurants, was an international byword for bland, dull cuisine, as it was to remain for several decades after Tennessee's visit to see the production.

The combination of unappealing factors, allied to his general preference for the sunshine and sexual liberality of the Continent, saw him pay Gielgud and his cast, headed by Helen Hayes as Amanda, the ultimate insult of leaving for Paris before the first night. Dogged by depression as he often was in life, and lonely as he felt without Salvatore's company and the familiar sights and sounds of Roman life, his behaviour could, on many more occasions than this, be strikingly rude and self-indulgent. The next year he was to repeat his flight from his commitments by missing the London opening of *A Streetcar Named Desire*. Given the long-standing professional rivalry between Gielgud and Olivier, perhaps he felt he had to avoid favouritism by being equally rude to both men.

Despite this, he was a big enough talent for people to put the playwright before the man and to welcome him back to London on many more occasions. He came because whatever his feelings about

Tennessee Williams on an ocean liner in 1952. As soon as he could afford to, he lived a transatlantic lifestyle, spending as much time as possible in Italy.

the British class system (still rigidly in place in the late 1940s, though losing its grip as the years passed and his new plays crossed the Atlantic), London was, and is, the world capital of theatre. Accordingly, Williams had a natural interest in and respect for it. And it is precisely because of the remnants of their class system that the British entirely 'get' those of his characters who belong to the faded gentry, down on their luck and living, with increasing desperation, in the past. They also like a star, and many major American actresses have travelled to London, whether to the National Theatre or to the West End, to act in his plays. Among the roll call have been Glenn Close, and more recently, Gillian Anderson, as Blanche DuBois in *A Streetcar Named Desire* and Lauren Bacall – and more recently, Kim Cattrall – as Alexandra Del Lago in *Sweet Bird of Youth*. In the latter, Miss Cattrall played

Vaslav Nijinsky, a central character in Tennessee Williams's *A Cavalier for Milady*, is seen here in the iconic title role, choreographed by him, of *L'Apres-midi d'un faune.*

opposite Seth Numrich, a young actor whose career in London and on Broadway has had the stellar trajectory Chance Wayne could only dream of.

London's unrivalled collection of playhouses mean that there are plenty of large, grand theatres in which to stage Tennessee's work, from the National Theatre on the South Bank to the Theatre Royal, Haymarket. London also has a very large and constantly expanding range of 'fringe' theatres (the Print Room in Notting Hill being a very recent example) in converted buildings ranging from pubs to disused swimming pools. These smaller spaces are ideal for imaginative stagings of Williams's later plays and have had an important part in the posthumous rehabilitation of Williams's lesser-known writing. Most recently, three of his plays, set in hotel rooms, were staged in a hotel in central London. The plays had mixed reviews but were universally welcomed as a chance to see previously unperformed work by America's greatest playwright.

A further sign of how his work continues to be explored and developed lies in the way it has been translated into different media. Due to the continuing popularity of *A Streetcar Named Desire*, it is not surprising that this piece is at the forefront of such treatment. In 1995 André Previn, one of the best-known conductors in the world, composed an opera version of *A Streetcar Named Desire* (libretto by Philip Littell), which premiered with the San Francisco Opera and has been seen in many cities in the United States as well as the United Kingdom, Ireland, France, Italy and Japan. More recently, the Scottish National Ballet has commissioned a dance version of the same play. Shaped by two women, director Nancy Meckler and choreographer Annabelle Lopez Ochoa, the result was a highly dramatic ballet that took the original and inspired decision to take Alan, Blanche's young husband, out of the shadows and onto the stage. He became an integral part of the dance story, his sexuality expressed by dancing with a male wedding guest as well as with Blanche on the day of their marriage. The rape scene between Stanley and Blanche was all the more distressing for being followed through, in dramatic choreography, at some length. Tennessee enjoyed dance, and his empathy with the fate of Vaslav Nijinsky, the star of the Ballets Russes before the First World War, has already been touched upon. In yet another case of one of his plays receiving a belated airing, Jermyn Street Theatre, in St James's, London, has staged *A Cavalier for Milady*, where a mentally disturbed young woman conjures up Nijinsky's spirit. When he refuses to have sex with her, not wanting to defile his status as an artist and the embodiment of dance, she finally gives up and orders, over the phone, a rent boy from an escort agency –

insisting to the agency that she will only accept a boy if the agency can find her one who looks like Nijinsky!

Other media have also contributed to the reinterpretation of Tennessee Williams's work. In 1992 an episode of *The Simpsons*, called *A Streetcar Named Marge*, saw Marge playing Blanche in a musical of *A Streetcar Named Desire*. In it, her husband Homer displays much of the casual uncouthness of Stanley but through watching Marge onstage comes to appreciate her all the more. A more conventional small-screen adaptation occurred some years later, when, in 2003, a TV film was made of Tennessee's novel *The Roman Spring of Mrs Stone*, with Helen Mirren playing Karen Stone, and the smoulderingly attractive Olivier Martinez as Paolo. Tennessee, who always preferred the theatre, would have been delighted that Martin Sherman, author of the groundbreaking play *Bent*, not only wrote the screenplay for the film of 2003, but also adapted the novella for the stage in a production that opened in Japan, where Williams's work has always had its fans. Williams had a reciprocal admiration for Japanese culture and two characters-come-stage hands who are a feature of *The Milk Train Doesn't Stop Here Anymore* show the direct influence of the Japanese dance/mime art form, Kabuki.

Though his plays belong to the world, Williams came from America, and it is in the United States that his memory is most cherished and kept alive. New York, the second greatest theatre city in the world, continues to be the natural platform for his plays, but three other areas where he lived and worked claim him as their own, sharing a pride in their association with him in life and promoting the study, celebration and performance of his work long after his death.

Starting with the furthest south, there is Key West. It was there, near the sea he loved so much (and at the closest point he could get to the site of Hart Crane's suicide) that, in 1950, he bought the house at 1431 Duncan Street that was to be the closest thing he had to a home for the rest of his life. Not far away is the Tennessee

Williams Key West Exhibit, a registered charity that has Williams memorabilia and promotes the study of his work, alongside events like film screenings and poetry competitions – the latter a tribute to his life-long love of verse. Next is New Orleans, the city most closely associated with him in the public imagination and to which he will always be linked, thanks to *A Streetcar Named Desire*. A book, *Tennessee Williams and the South*, co-authored by Kenneth Holditch and Richard Freeman Leavitt and published by the University Press of Mississippi, goes into considerable and fascinating detail about what the writers refer to as the 'astounding' number of places he lived in, from slums to smart hotels to the house that he bought on Dumaine Street, in New Orleans. Tennessee Williams is, naturally, part of the literary tourist trail. Among the businesses that also make reference to his plays are a cycle hire company called A Bicycle Named Desire and a restaurant called Stella! Stella! This comes from Stanley Kowalski's anguished cries of 'Stella!' after his wife seeks temporary refuge in her neighbour's flat. The 'Stella!' contest, where participants vie for the loudest, most impressive impersonation of Marlon Brando's screen performance of the cry, is one of the most popular parts of New Orleans' annual Tennessee Williams Festival, held over several days around the anniversary of his birth on 26 March.

The most northerly place to celebrate this most Southern of writers is Provincetown, Massachusetts, on whose dunes Williams had sex with Kip Kiernan and which he immortalized in *Something Cloudy, Something Clear.* Established in 2006, this has become a major annual event for scholars and fans. It hosts several days of plays, films, lectures and seminars every September, combining serious admiration for its subject with a sense of fun. Fun is something one might not immediately associate with the anguished heroines and frustrated characters Williams created, but the sense of hope, human sympathy and the resilience he showed in his own life lend themselves to celebration rather than mourning. As a famous playwright, he was photographed time and again over several decades. There are some where he looks bereft or bored, notably a snap taken on the film set of *Boom!*, which shows an amusingly dysfunctional-looking group, their negative body language matched by the bored, vacant (and possibly stoned) face of Williams turned away from an evidently ill-at-ease Elizabeth Taylor. But a great many other photos show him laughing, affectionately holding the arms of (usually women) friends and enjoying people's company. These photos seem to say, 'Don't feel sorry for me.'

This is understandable because, while his plays deal with the damaged and the doomed, they also contain a message of hope and a facility to find poetry in the most unlikely and unpromising situations. They are the shimmering embodiment of a need to embrace life, to enjoy it where possible and to defy anything that stands in its way. At all events, and however overwhelming the circumstances, life is not just to be endured, but to be made the most of. It was Tennessee Williams's gift that he was able to turn his own life – tragic, neurotic, damaged, volatile, promiscuous, well travelled, exuberant – into art. Whether in the form of fiction, poetry or drama, that art continues to enhance our lives, just as it gave meaning, shape and solace to his. It was powered by a determination, however much he mined the past, to face the future and move forward into it. That determination was summed up in the two-word French phrase that he frequently addressed to himself, his friends and lovers – a mantra as appropriate to his reverses as to his many and richly deserved triumphs. It applies equally to the way new generations of theatregoers continue to enjoy his talent long after he has left the stage: 'En avant!'

Selected Plays

Williams wrote scores of plays in his life, some of which are still being discovered and many of which appeared in various forms over the years. This is a personal selection of the most interesting or significant ones.

1935   *Cairo! Shanghai! Bombay!*: Of note as his first (co-written) play.

1937   *Candles to the Sun*: His first full-length play – a political piece set during a miners' strike.

1938   *Not About Nightingales*: A political drama set in a brutal prison.

1940   *Battle of Angels*: A disastrous Boston production of this melodrama lasts just two weeks.

1941   *Moony's Kid Don't Cry*: His first (one-act) play published. The central character is a poor, handsome, working-class man whose life has not lived up to his dreams.

1943   *You Touched Me!*: Co-written with his friend Donald Windham. A typical theme of the conflict between higher aims and carnal desire, but very untypically set in an English country house.

1944   *The Glass Menagerie*: Opens in Chicago, transfers to Broadway the next year. Very autobiographical family drama with the most direct portrayal in all his work of his sister Rose – in the character of Laura.

1947   *A Streetcar Named Desire*: This play had a Broadway opening and is still his best-known play, with a plot involving the decline of the Old South, brutal sex and mental illness.

1948   *Summer and Smoke*: A drama about the overriding need for even 'high-minded' people to recognize the power of sexual desire has its short Broadway run. The play is not a success until its revival in 1952.

1951   *The Rose Tattoo*: Tennessee's affectionate take on Italian-American culture.

1953   *Camino Real*: A difficult, dreamlike play that quickly closed. It features real-life characters as well as fictional ones and is set in a nightmarish, isolated town somewhere in South America.

1955   *Cat on a Hot Tin Roof*: A blistering family drama set in the Deep South.

1957   *Orpheus Descending*: An improved version of *Battle of Angels*. A dangerously attractive young man's arrival in a small town sets off a chain of events that leads to his and his lover's violent deaths.

1958   *Suddenly Last Summer*: Along with the rarely performed and understated *Something Unspoken*, this was part of a double bill presented as *Garden District*. Both plays are about illicit love: *Suddenly Last Summer* is his most melodramatic play; *Something Unspoken* one of his gentlest.

1959   *Sweet Bird of Youth*: Another take on the horrors of growing old and thwarted dreams, involving a formerly beautiful gigolo and an ageing Hollywood film star, against a background of the violence and corruption of the Deep South.

1960   *Period of Adjustment*: A comedy about marriage with a lightness of touch, in dramatic contrast to most of Williams's classic plays.

1961   *The Night of the Iguana*: His last major Broadway hit, set on the Mexican coast and featuring an unfrocked priest, a ballsy female hotel owner and the world's oldest working poet.

1963   *The Milk Train Doesn't Stop Here Anymore*: Set on the Italian coast that Williams and his friends (especially Gore Vidal) enjoyed so much, this has a wealthy, dying widow and a hippy-like young poet who arrives at her villa and stays until her death.

1966   *The Mutilated* and *The Gnadiges Fraulein*: One-act plays presented together as *Slapstick Tragedy*. The run lasts a week. Both plays involve physically deformed women who are made outcasts by society. They show a more nightmarish take on life than usual, but one that was in tune with the weirder, drug-influenced style of the 1960s.

1967   *The Two-character Play*: London saw the first outing for this often reworked play, set in a theatre and focusing on sibling relationships and madness, two of his classic themes.

1968 *Kingdom of Earth* (also known as *The Seven Descents of Myrtle*):
      This drama involving family tensions, madness and the survival
      of the fittest is first performed. Similar, despite the different setting,
      to his much more successful *A Streetcar Named Desire*.

1969 *In the Bar of a Tokyo Hotel*: Though this only ran for a few weeks, it is
      a good example of his underrated later work, with, as often, the best
      role being that of the central female character.

1972 *Small Craft Warnings*: Moderately successful, not least because the
      playwright appeared on stage in a rare acting role, this is set in a bar
      where a group of misfits drift through. Haunted by the memory of
      a young, dead, gay man – again, shades of *A Streetcar Named Desire*.

1976 *The Red Devil Battery Sign*: A political drama, set in Dallas and
      involving violent revolutionaries. It failed to attract audiences.

1977 *Vieux Carré*: Another failure, but a fascinating play that has enjoyed
      subsequent revivals. Its central character is the young Tennessee
      Williams, and it is set in the New Orleans boarding house where
      the writer lived early in his career.

1979 *A Lovely Sunday for Creve Coeur*: Another late play that shows
      Williams's artistry was still alive, despite critical attacks and self-
      destructive behaviour. Set in an apartment and with an all-female cast,
      it has the feel of the 1960s, despite belonging to the end of the 1970s.

1980 *Clothes for a Summer Hotel*: Williams's take on the doomed marriage
      of Zelda and Scott Fitzgerald, it was slammed by the critics but is
      another example of how his late work is far better written than it
      was given credit for when first performed.

1981 *Something Cloudy, Something Clear*: Highly autobiographical with
      a self-loathing twist, this is a memory play set in the coastal resort
      of Provincetown, both in 1940 (when he had a real-life romance
      there) and in the present day.

1982 *A House Not Meant to Stand*: This striking comedy with a
      melancholy subtext has a Chicago run. Family hatreds, the
      fundamental human need for love, the bitterness caused by poverty,
      the urgings of the sex drive, nostalgia for the past and the enduring
      power of a mother's love – here presented as something positive,
      unlike the warped version of the same emotion in *Suddenly Last
      Summer* – all coalesce in an extraordinary late play.

Select Bibliography

Bak, John S., ed., *Tennessee Williams: New Selected Essays: Where I Live*
    (New York, 2009)
Holditch, Kenneth, and Richard Freeman Leavitt, *Tennessee Williams and*
    the South (Jackson, MI, 2002)
Kaplan, David, ed., *Tenn at One Hundred: The Reputation of Tennessee*
    Williams (East Brunswick, NJ, 2011)
Kaplan, Fred, *Gore Vidal* (London, 1999)
Lahr, John, *Tennessee Williams: Mad Pilgrimage of the Flesh* (New York, 2014)
Murphy, Brenda, *The Theatre of Tennessee Williams* (London, 2014)
—, *Tennessee Williams and Elia Kazan: A Collaboration in Theatre*
    (Cambridge, 1992)
Narducci, Tony, *In the Frightened Heart of Me: Tennessee Williams's Last Year*
    (Bloomington, IN, 2013)
Parini, Jay, *Every Time a Friend Succeeds Something Inside Me Dies*
    (New York, 2015)
Rader, Dotson, *Tennessee Williams: An Intimate Memoir* (London, 1985)
Roessel, David, and Nicholas Moschovakis, eds, *The Collected Poems of*
    Tennessee Williams (New York, 2002)
Roudané, Matthew C., ed., *The Cambridge Companion to Tennessee Williams*
    (Cambridge, 1997)
Simon, Marc, ed., *The Complete Poems of Hart Crane* (New York, 1986)
Smith-Howard, Alycia, and Greta Heintzelman, *Critical Companion to*
    Tennessee Williams (New York, 2005)
Spoto, Donald, *The Kindness of Strangers: The Life of Tennessee Williams*
    (New York, 1985)
Thornton, Margaret Bradham, ed., *Tennessee Williams: Notebooks*
    (New Haven, CT, and London, 2006)

Williams, Tennessee, *Memoirs* (New York, 1975)

—, *The Roman Spring of Mrs Stone* (London, 1999)

—, *Collected Stories*, intro. Gore Vidal (New York, 1980)

—, 'The Man in the Overstuffed Chair', in *Tennessee Williams: New Selected Essays: Where I Live*, ed. John S. Bak (New York, 2009), pp. 97–106

Acknowledgements

I would like to thank my editor at Reaktion Books, Ben Hayes, for commissioning this work and for his calm, good-humoured help through the process of moving from initial idea to printed page – especially as this took longer than either of us anticipated . . .

I would also like to thank Jill and John Broome and Carol and Craig Rossiter for their hospitality when I started this project, as well as Pip Pickering, as ever, for his friendship and constructive criticism.

Finally, and above all, I am hugely grateful to Tom Erhardt for his support, knowledge and encouragement to write on a subject on which he is, having been Tennessee Williams's play agent in Europe for several decades, a wise and generous expert.

PERMISSIONS

For permission to quote excerpts of the poems 'We Have Not Long to Love', 'Little Horse', 'Those Who Ignore', 'Youth Must Be Wanton', 'Cried the Fox', 'The Blond Mediterraneans', 'They That Come Late to the Dance', 'Life Story' and 'Covenant' by Tennessee Williams, from *The Collected Poems of Tennessee Williams*, copyright © 1925, 1926, 1932, 1933, 1935, 1936, 1937, 1938, 1939, 1942, 1944, 1947, 1948, 1949, 1950, 1952, 1956, 1960, 1961, 1963, 1964, 1971, 1975, 1977, 1978, 1979, 1981, 1982, 1983, 1991, 1995, 2002 by The University of the South, reprinted by permission of New Directions Publishing Corp.

Photo Acknowledgements

The author and publishers wish to express their thanks to the below sources of illustrative material and/or permission to reproduce it.

Photo © Alamy: pp. 73, 88, 96, 97; © Bettmann/Corbis: p. 102; photograph courtesy of Sheila Burnett: p. 124; © Condé Nast Archive/Corbis: p. 78; photo © Getty Images: pp. 17, 110, 116, 134, 149, 165, 174, 179, 180; photos photography collection, Harry Ransom Center, The University of Texas at Austin: pp. 12, 24, 26; courtesy of Tamara Harvey: p. 157; courtesy of Shinji Hosono: p. 91; photo by Douglas H. Jeffrey at Victoria and Albert Museum, Theatre and Performance, London: p. 42; Library of Congress Prints and Photographs Division, *New York World-Telegram* and the *Sun* newspaper photograph collection, Washington, DC: pp. 6, 65, 85, 129; courtesy of Tim Medley: p. 140; courtesy of Victoria and Albert Museum, Theatre and Performance, London: p. 109.